Child of Rage

by
Glenn Hester
and
Bruce Nygren

THOMAS NELSON PUBLISHERS
Nashville

Published in Nashville, Tennessee, by Thomas Nelson, Inc., Publishers and distributed in Canada by Lawson Falle, Ltd., Cambridge, Ontario.

Printed in the United States of America.

Sources for statistics and background information include:

Chapter 9

"Hospital Attendants Fined in Beating Death of Patient," *Roanoke Times,* Sept. 25, 1965.

"Millions Needed to Upgrade State Mental Health Program," *Roanoke Times,* Oct. 21, 1965.

Chapter 16

"Who Knows? Who Cares? Forgotten Children in Foster Care," 1979 Report of the National Commission on Children in Need of Parents, 801 2nd Ave., New York, N. Y. 10017.

"Redirecting Foster Care. A Report to the Mayor of the City of New York," prepared by the Mayor's Task Force on Foster Care Services, June, 1980.

"Nobody's Children," script from *ABC News Closeup,* broadcast Dec. 28, 1979.

"Foster Care Once Again Is Enveloped in Scandal," *The New York Times,* Oct. 14, 1979.

Other

Children Without Homes, report issued by the Children's Defense Fund 1978, 1520 New Hampshire Ave., N. W., Washington, D. C. 20036.

Library of Congress Cataloging in Publication Data

Hester, Glenn M.
    Child of rage.

    1. Hester, Glenn M.   2. Converts—United States
—Biography.   3. Foster home care—United States.
I. Nygren, Bruce A.   II. Title.
BV4935.H49A33   287'.97   [B]   81-9490
ISBN 0-8407-5245-8   AACR2

For all the children
who have been killed
or abused in foster
care and institutions.

Acknowledgments

Thanks to: Brooke McAdam, Jill Rappaport, and Kenneth Quigg for professional guidance; Stephen and Caren Urgolites and Mr. and Mrs. James Carroll—among many others—for their love and concern; friends of the Waynesboro and Brooklyn Free Methodist churches, the Church of God, and Christian Retreats for their support; my aunt; my mother—for whom I have a special love; and Carla for hanging on.

—Glenn Hester
Brooklyn
January, 1981

Thanks to: Glenn and Carla Hester for the story and warm hospitality; Racinda and Noelle Nygren for patience and support; Roberta Aves for typing; and my friends at Thomas Nelson for the opportunity to write.

A special thank you to my parents, Florence and Edwin, for giving me the type of childhood Glenn longed to have.

—Bruce Nygren
Nashville
January, 1981

Contents

This story is true.
Some names have been changed
and some details of incidents altered
to preserve the anonymity
of persons living or dead.

Prologue

Waynesboro, Virginia, June 30, 1973

The hands on the wall clock show 11:03 P.M. I have decided to kill someone tonight.

Alone in the living room, I am submerged in a stuffed chair staring at the television screen. A fan pushes heavy, warm air across the room, nudging my hair. My shirt, moist from perspiration, is matted between my back and the plastic cushion. The TV program that convinced me I should kill Brandon White is over.

Just another Saturday night. Willie and John are out. The party in Charlottesville is rolling now; *I could be there, drinking, on the make. It's still early. I can go there after I shoot Brandon White.*

A fat, black fly buzzes over my head, diving and rolling back and forth. I swing my hand wildly at him, swearing.

I've not killed before. There are many I've wanted to kill who deserve to die . . . I see their faces staring at me, blaming me, hating me. Why haven't I killed before? Plenty of chances. I've cut flesh with my knives and felt warm blood on my fists.

The television blinks at me in vain. I'm no longer tuned in. Thoughts weave through my mind, twisted as always. Nothing makes sense.

That program on TV gave me some useful information. . . . A guy killed a man and was sentenced to ten years in the joint. Six years later he was paroled and put back on the street. He murdered a guy and in six years he was free! They want to lock me up for five years for just threatening to kill Brandon White? Why don't I shoot him and end up with

9

six? What's one more stinking year in jail matter when you can get even?

I may die soon. Maybe I should help myself die. But I'm only twenty-five years old. Tears brim in my eyes, but before they fall, I pull myself up in the chair and grab the can from the low table before me. The warm beer flows in a stream down my throat, but after three days of alcohol my taste is dead.

I must think clearly now—hold my mind on this plan to kill. The rifle and the shotgun stand in the corner. The loaded automatic pistol is on the table near my feet. *I will need these and the other guns in the car. Do I have enough shells? Yes . . . bought plenty at the hardware store two weeks ago. The boxes are in the car trunk.*

My heart pounds. Blood rushes through my head, hissing in my ears. *Can I pull the trigger on a man? Can I hear the shell roar and watch him crumple, see his longings and memories slipping away?*

My hands shake, the tears stand hot in my eyes. An ache spreads through my forehead. I feel the fear again, fluttering in my stomach and throat. Always, always the fear. I almost laugh, then say aloud: "Here I am, the toughest guy on earth, afraid!"

I must do something.

Two months have passed since Brandon White and his friends humiliated me in the bar, called me yellow. After that I mailed Brandon a note telling him that when he pulled the little scene in the bar, he signed his death warrant. White called the police and the FBI.

Some FBI agents came to me with their questions. Then the probation officer, who said I would probably get five years in prison for sending a death threat through the mail. The trial starts in ten days.

Brandon White is laughing at me. That's a dangerous thing to do. He's keeping Arlene away from me. He's pushed me. Nobody pushes Glenn Hester. I'm going to go to prison for just saying I'd kill him. I might as well do it and stop his laughing.

11:30. *I should go. . . . One more cigarette.* I light up, draw deeply, lean back. Through the haze I look at myself: Feet are bare, the toenails long and jagged; jeans are spotted with red dirt and grease; undershirt, yellowed from spilled beer and sweat, is spotted with automobile grease and dried blood. My face is puffy, roughened by a five-day beard. My hair, thinning at the temples, is stringy and damp. I smell myself; I stink.

I remove my eyeglasses. The thick lenses are clouded by dried sweat and tears.

Staring at the glasses, I remember again my months at Spofford, the jail for juveniles in New York City . . .

I need new glasses, my eyes have weakened. I move blindly, shifting my head from side to side, squinting to catch the glint of a knife blade or flash of a fist aimed at my head. There are hundreds, maybe thousands of teen-agers in here, spilling blood and learning the ABCs of violence and crime. *Those idiot social workers think I'm nervous, always jerking my head from side to side. I'm not nervous; I can't see well, even with glasses! I could get killed here and not even see how it happened.*

Spofford. I should have killed some people there . . . like the guard who tried to use my body, the one who finally turned his back on me. I grabbed the chair and crashed it against his skull. The other guards came with their clubs and beat me. They said I was crazy. I was sent to the mental hospital. But the guard—he paid . . .

11:40. The shotgun, black and oiled, rests tenderly in my arms. I cock the hammer three times; the trigger snaps hard and clean. *I love guns. I love their power. I love the power they give me . . . but why do I feel so small and weak? And afraid?*

Why, always, the fear? Was I afraid even in Mother's womb? Did I sense that I was unwanted, unloved—forever fatherless and homeless? Always to be alone?

The TV flashes on and on, the black and white shadows

bouncing from the tile floor. Tired of the noise, I rise and turn it off—jabbing the switch with the butt of my gun. In the quiet I notice the ringing in my ears. My legs tremble. *When did I eat last?* I light another cigarette. Sweat beads grow on my forehead. *The heat! The stinking summer Virginia heat.* I remember a summer day long ago in Queens . . .

The sun is warm but not hot. I am eight years old, whimpering as I ride in the lady social worker's car. "Stop your crying, Glenn!" the woman snaps. I try to quench my sobs, but the pain inside won't let me. I just said good-bye to Mother Winston. Tonight I'll sleep at the orphanage. I don't have a mommy and daddy anymore . . .

12:15 A.M. The shotgun, the pistol, the other guns and shells I've hauled to the car. I stand in the kitchen, a cigarette drooping from my lips. Amid the dirty dishes and rotting food on the kitchen counter, I find a can of beer. The opener snaps a hole in the top; I drink, long thirstless swallows. Three grocery sacks, overflowing with garbage, sag damply in the corner. A cobweb encircles a hanging light fixture. The sight draws my smile. "If the boys at the mental hospitals could see this!" I say with a quick laugh.

There, every surface was dusted, broomed, mopped, wiped, waxed, sterilized all day, every day, forever. No cobwebs, no dust in corners, no dirty clothes, no three-day-old newspapers—just Thorazine injections, clubs, hand cuffs, chains, and brutality. *Some people there need to be killed, too.*

My God, if I kill Brandon White, will they send me back to the nuthouse for criminals? The thought sobers me; chills walk down my back. *In that last insane asylum, where they tried to break and destroy me, my fear and hate hardened, hard as steel.*

12:20. I click off the kitchen light and pull the outside door shut. It is a little cooler now, the air made softly fragrant by flowering trees and freshly mown grass. *A lovely night after all. Can I kill a man on such a lovely night?*

The car engine starts smoothly. I pull away, looking back at the house. *Will I see this place again?*

In minutes I roll up the ramp to Interstate 64. The highway is serene, only an occasional car passing in either direction. As I drive, the memories, the plans, the fears in my mind unravel. *How can I lure Brandon White outside of his cabin? Why am I doing this? Where will I hide after the murder? Why am I afraid? Where should I leave the car? Did I turn off the bedroom light? Why didn't Mother care? Should I use the shotgun or pistol? What will I buy my son for his birthday? What if I can't pull the trigger? Do I want to die? Will they do the shock treatments this time? God, do you, does anybody care?*

12:30. Several miles further now. A few lights, dimmed by trees, glint from houses back on the hills. *I am so alone, so desperately alone.*

The tears come again. This time even my curses can't stop them, and they flow in angry rivers. A faint cry gathers in my throat. "Oh, God, I need help, some peace. Please."

The highway ribbons before me, clean, quiet, desolate. Ahead a green exit sign reflects the headlights. My hands strangle the wheel. I'm not sure anymore what I might do and how my life will end.

1. Nobody's Son

Baltimore, Maryland, the 1940s

I greeted life like everybody else—with a clean slate, crying out for love.

I was born on April 10, 1948. Years later, when I received a copy of my father's death certificate in the mail, I learned that he too had been born on that date. I wonder what he thought, becoming the father of a bastard son on his thirty-fifth birthday.

I may have seen my father once, but I don't remember. He would have been a stranger. Even though he and Mother combined to bring me life, he was married to another woman and never knew me, never held me in his arms. Ten days before Christmas, 1954, when I was seven years old, he pulled his car behind the house where he lived, ran a hose from the exhaust, and killed himself.

My mother was twenty-four when she had me, her first child. She's never told me if having an illegitimate child shamed her. I believe her hope for a happy, normal life was dead long before her unwanted child arrived.

Mother's early life was joyless and damaging. She grew up in North Carolina, near Durham. The family was poor, a white trash brood struggling to make ends meet in the Depression. There were two older brothers and my mother. Their father died when Mother was five, and the family's bleak life worsened. Desperate, my grandmother moved with the children to Baltimore, believing work and a better life awaited.

She was wrong. Things didn't work out, and it was worse being poor in an unknown city. The woman struggled to keep the family together, and I suppose the strain of just trying to stay alive drained her emotions dry. She and my mother didn't get along, always fussing and snapping at each other. My mother had already lost her daddy, and her mother was too tired, too whipped by misfortune to reach out in love. Mother was eleven when the family broke apart.

The three children were dumped at an orphanage. There they had food, warm clothing, and a bed; but the home's atmosphere was sterile, tense, and regimented. Love was scarce. I found too, years later, that love doesn't flourish in an institution where people are paid to give it.

Mother stayed in school until the end of tenth grade. For a while afterwards she studied to be a beauty operator, but then, because of World War II, she joined other women working in a defense plant, a piston factory.

The details of how my father and mother met and formed their relationship are known by someone I'm sure, but I've never cared to learn them. My mother, lonely, longing for the love and attention her parents and an institution could not give, must have been hungry for a loving look and embrace. She found both with a thirty-four-year-old married man.

Some weeks before my birth, I'm told, a woman knocked on the door of my uncle's house where my mother was staying, counting the days until her release from pregnancy. The woman, a stranger, peered through the doorway and asked for my mother, who happened to be away. Disappointed, the lady blurted out a message: "Tell that woman to stay away from my husband." She left, hurrying down the street, never to be seen again.

This must have been my father's wife. I think Mother took the message to heart and never saw my father again.

After I was born, Mother soon tired of parental duties. I was a month old when she abruptly left for New York City, leaving me with her older brother, Hank, and his wife, Sarah. She didn't say when she would be back. Mother never has said why she ran away from me. Maybe she didn't want to be an adult yet. Poverty and neglect had stolen her own childhood; I think she was young and wanted to taste some freedom, to see the world.

Months passed. I ate, slept, messed my diaper, got sick like any kid. Hank and Sarah grew to love me and wanted me to stay, to be their child. I had a home, a family. No letters came from Mother.

When I was thirteen months old, Mother returned, offering no explanation and showing no remorse. She had been gone a year. I could have stayed in Baltimore where I was warm and loved, but Mother wanted her little Glenn right away.

How did my aunt and uncle feel after a year of caring, walking floors, giving love—a way of life, all changed in a moment by a young woman's whim?

I suppose they cried when their baby boy left and wondered if Mother would bring him back in a few days or weeks. She did send me back, finally, fifteen years later, a hardened, seething teen-ager, full of hate.

Mother took me by train to New York City where my new baby brother waited. Mother had forgotten to tell the folks in Baltimore that she had borne another child while she was gone.

Before long Mother again grew weary of parenting. The man she was living with was a gambler, an impulsive, violent man. I doubt he wanted to play daddy for two baby boys. While Mother tried to untangle her own life, my brother Stanley and I were placed temporarily in a foundling hospital. Mother was repeating the cycle of her own life. Only this time she was the adult—withholding, robbing her children of affection.

Mother came and took us from the hospital after a short time, but then some other crisis interrupted, and we were dumped again. Stanley and I never stayed anywhere for long. By the time I was three, we had already lived in four institutions. And the New York Board of Welfare was our official custodian. We were like runty pups in a litter. No home could be found for us, but we were too cute to destroy.

Now I watch little kids, how they run to mommy's arms

and fall asleep on daddy's shoulder. I've seen them laughing at the supper table, sleeping in a carriage on a busy street—so unaware that anything could be wrong in the world because they are safe in a warm, cozy little kingdom.

I had no mommy and daddy like that. Just one set of stiff, white-uniformed, different-feeling arms after another. I know many of those people cared, even loved. But there were too many of them, too many changing faces and voices and arms, and not one face, not one voice, not one enfolding embrace was mine. All mine.

I was just a toddling baby when the tenderness inside me began to die. I have no early dreams of laughter and warmth. I only remember feeling alone. Alone and afraid.

2. Foster Child

New York City, the 1950s

I was three years old when I went to live with a real mommy and daddy. The memory is clouded, but I can recall the day, a blistering July afternoon.

The lady social worker came to the group home for Stanley and me. While she signed the papers and packed our few clothes and toys in a box, I scampered across the yard and looked up in awe at her car. The automobile seemed huge and exciting. Cautiously I climbed up on the car's running board and peeked inside. The cloth-covered seats were thick and soft, the interior clean. I smiled as I thought about riding in such a machine.

The social worker loaded us, locked the doors, and rolled down the windows. Then we drove for miles, to the edge of the city, to Middle Village Queens. As we turned down the street of our new home, in the distance I could see a farmer on a tractor cutting hay.

The car stopped in front of a medium-sized, brick home. Before we could step out, our foster parents came quickly down the front steps to the walk. They were smiling and eager. I saw other adults and children moving excitedly our way. My new mommy and daddy, Anita and John Winston, lifted us from the car. Mrs. Winston kissed us both and laughed in a nervous, happy way. Their daughter Caroline, a bobby-soxed teen-ager, said: "Look at my two little brothers!" Charles, her older brother and also in high school, looked on, grinning broadly.

Stanley and I were passed from one friendly set of arms to another. I knew we were welcome. I felt warm inside.

When we entered the house, we were met boisterously at

the door by a small white dog. "Her name is Chrissie," Caroline said, kneeling to greet the dog. "Do you want to pet her?" Stanley and I were timid at first. We had never played with a puppy. But Chrissie's evident goodwill won us over, and we patted her head and back.

The social worker brought out the papers for signing and gave the Winstons—and the two of us—her official, stern-faced parting words. Then she left, her huge car purring down the street. The neighbors drifted away too and, shyly at first, we explored our new home. Chrissie sniffed through all the rooms with us.

The house seemed immense to me, one mysterious room leading to another. My little-boy eyes didn't see it as it was, a basic, middle-class house—three or four bedrooms, a bath, living and dining rooms, kitchen, and full basement. In back was a modest yard, although the grassy area seemed the size of a park to my small feet.

The Winstons were solid, hard-working people who in their middle years wanted to share their love again with small children. Mr. Winston worked for the electric company. Mrs. Winston was a housewife who happily found time to care for us.

The day-to-day patterns of any normal child's life emerged—eating, play, some spankings, bedtime prayers, sleep. In a few days we were calling the Winstons Mommy and Daddy. At age three I didn't dwell on the legal differences between natural and foster parents. I lived in a house with a woman and man I called Mommy and Daddy. The mommy kissed my bruises, and the daddy set me on his lap and rubbed his knobby, hard hands across the top of my head. They loved me; I loved them; I had a home.

Making her rounds, the social worker would stop now and then. She would sit near us on the living room couch, looking Stanley and me over from the corner of her eye, searching for any unusual scrapes or bruises while she and Mrs. Winston chatted about how we were eating and behaving. These visits meant little to me, only a moment's interruption in the endless, happy hours of a child's life.

Many young families, each with three or four kids, lived in the neighborhood. My brother and I found playmates with whom we ran and chased on the quiet streets. There were many trees, tall shady ones that even little boys could climb.

Sometimes Mrs. Winston would take me along on her errands. I would wear my Brooklyn Dodgers' baseball cap and my Davy Crockett tee shirt. At the bank the teller would hand me a lollipop, and at the meat shop the butcher would cut me a thick slice of bologna—all this for just being a kid and belonging to someone.

At holiday times, Caroline would dress Stanley and me in costumes. On Halloween we might be gypsies, at Thanksgiving Indians or pilgrims.

On Saturday nights Mother put both of us in the bathtub and scrubbed until we shined. We splashed and shrieked with delight. We had to be clean for Sunday. Every week the whole family attended a Lutheran church.

There were some darker moments, of course. My brother and I fought, like most boys near in age do. Being a year younger, Stanley was still baby-cute and affectionate. Neighbors and friends of the Winstons who visited hugged him more than me. I became jealous and insecure, and released my anger by turning on Stanley with my fists.

Our fights would continue over the years. Stanley's more cooperative, quiet personality kept him out of trouble and brought him affection. I was excitable, mouthy, rebellious—a loner who showed insecurity in a manner that troubled and disgusted adults. Stanley would be hugged; I would be spanked. I wanted so much to be loved, but I felt helpless in changing my behavior. So in frustration I lashed out at my brother, and the punishment which followed reinforced my sense of rejection. It was the same story over and over.

Two years passed at the Winstons without any word from my real mother. Then one summer afternoon when I was five, she drifted ominously back into my life, like a quick-rising summer thunderstorm. I was tossing a beach ball in the backyard when Mrs. Winston called, "Glenn! Come, Glenn, your mother is here to see you."

I was puzzled, aware that my heart had begun to pound. I could not understand why the mommy I lived with would call some other woman "mother." Fear flooded my chest.

Dragging my feet, I stumbled warily inside, finding there an overweight woman wearing a bright orange dress. An unpleasant odor of perfume hung damply in the room. The lady smiled broadly and giggled as she gathered her "darling little boys" into her large arms. She called herself my mother and spoke excitedly of her new life and her plans to take her boys home, home to be with her.

I was terrified. The fear of losing my home with the Winstons threatened to unloose sobs at any moment. When the woman left two hours later, I was trembling. Mother Winston held me close, but not even her arms could dim my fear.

Mother's visits continued, and each one had the same effect on me. When they ended, I would find Mrs. Winston and cry deeply and long. She would hold and comfort me. I know now that we were holding and comforting each other; Mrs. Winston was afraid too, fearful she might lose her little boys.

Sometimes the social worker would come after Mother's visits. "Glenn, you mustn't get so upset when your mother visits. You're a big boy now," she would say. This is my earliest memory of a professional counselor making me feel guilty for expressing normal emotions. Did this tired old social worker playing psychologist really expect a small child not to be upset by the possibility of losing his home?

Mrs. Winston, tired of spending days soothing my fears after each of Mother's visits, asked the social worker to stop them—in particular since Mother was bringing her latest boyfriend along, an ex-convict who cursed heavily. I was relieved not to see her anymore. She had become an enemy, a threat to my security.

When I was five, the foster care agency Stanley and I were placed by closed down, and another local private agency took over. The Winstons, tired of the trauma caused by Mother's erratic behavior and wanting to stabilize their lives, began to think seriously about adopting my brother and me.

Repeatedly they inquired if we could be adopted. The answer always was no. Supposedly we were not available for adoption. Years later I learned that in fact we had been available, but for unspecified reasons the agency didn't want the Winstons to have us.

This dealing over us went on without my knowledge—my life of playing, eating, and sleeping continued without interruption. By the summer of 1953, as the warm days passed, I was as eager as any child to start first grade in the fall. Franklin Elementary School was only a block from our house.

The first day of school, I squirmed like all the other kids while seated at my desk. I recognized some of my playmates, though there were many kids I didn't know. My excitement rose as the teacher, a tall, serious-looking woman in her mid-forties, tried to subdue the surging energy of her class. When she finally said "Boys and girls!" in a loud voice, a deep hush fell on the room.

"My name is Mrs. Spanogla. Welcome to first grade. I'll be your teacher this year. Now, girls and boys, I want each of you to stand up at your desk—one at a time!—and tell the others your name. No other talking, *please!*"

My turn came and, standing with a bounce, I blurted, "My name is Glenn Winston."

The teacher's eyes narrowed, and the smile on her face faded. She stepped several feet nearer my desk and said firmly, almost accusingly, "Your name is not Glenn Winston. Your name is Glenn Hester."

I began to protest, but she moved even closer, towering above me. "Your name is Glenn Hester. You don't belong to the Winstons. You are a foster child."

The room was still. Dozens of small eyes pierced me with puzzled looks. A boy in the back of the room giggled. Shame seeped through me; I could feel its icy warmth crawling up my legs, spreading along my stomach and back, rising to a bloody hue in my face.

I'll never forget that moment. It erupts from my memory, a monument marking the early stirrings of my hate and humiliation. I sometimes dream of that first day in school, the adult, the bearer of authority, towering over me, pointing me out, making me different. I learned that day I couldn't just be Glenn anymore, the little boy who lived with Mom and Dad Winston. I had to be Glenn Hester, the foster child, the bastard, the kid who belonged to nobody.

From that day my troubles mounted. For the first time I knew for certain what I had only feared before: I was an outsider.

3. She Doesn't Love You

Queens, the 1950s

Having learned what I was made me feel different and somehow dirty. I began to struggle for an identity, using rowdy behavior in school as my way of seeking attention and love.

My speaking out of turn and loud disruptions of the class turned Mrs. Spanogla into an enemy. I lied to her and provoked my classmates by calling them names and tearing up their books and papers. I was jealous of their homes, their parents. I hated their taunts about my being a foster child with two names.

Our social worker learned of my behavior at school and sent me to a psychologist. He talked to me and decided that my insecurity had sprouted years before when Mother and the board of welfare were passing me from place to place. Even a baby can know what homelessness feels like.

Mom and Dad Winston went on loving me, trying to help me adjust and feel that I belonged. They made a desperate, final attempt to adopt my brother and me. In the process they made a tragic mistake.

After gathering some money, they contacted my mother directly and offered four thousand dollars for Stanley and me. She agreed to the terms. A lawyer was hired so the deal would be tidy and legal. But before the court could transfer us to the Winstons permanently, the foster care agency had to be contacted and their permission given. I don't know the details, but the deal fell apart. My mother lost the chance for four thousand dollars, and I lost my hope for a normal home and a single name—Glenn Winston.

I was not, of course, included in the negotiations. I do remember, though, one incident that frightened me and I suppose warned me intuitively of sad days ahead. One morning, after playing Davy Crockett with a friend who lived several houses down the block, I ran into the house and found Mother Winston sitting at the dining room table crying. Her eyes were reddened, her cheeks streaked with tears. I approached her carefully, placing my small arms around her waist, hoping to comfort her. "What's wrong?" I asked, my own wobbling voice betraying fear and insecurity.

Mrs. Winston did not look at me; she just pushed me gently aside with one arm. "Go away now, I'm too upset," she said. I left, shaken and afraid.

The Winstons had just learned the foster care agency had declared them unfit and neglectful. They were no longer eligible to be foster parents.

I have never verified why the Winstons were dropped. I believe it happened because they violated the first commandment of a foster care agency: "Foster parents must never deal directly with the natural parent in an adoption proceeding."

After a five-year stay, our bags were packed—again— with some clothes, several pairs of shoes, and a few toys and trinkets. The morning Stanley and I left, Mrs. Winston fed us breakfast and gave us fresh clothing. We were waiting soberly in the living room when the social worker arrived.

I carried my bag to the sidewalk. It was June, and the voices of children at play sounded up and down the street. I stood near the car. Inside, Mrs. Winston signed papers. When she and the social worker walked down the stoop, I began to cry, whimpering at first, then sobbing. The two women tried to hold and calm me, but I pushed and strained away. My heart was full of pain. I remember seeing Mrs. Winston as we drove away; she waved weakly, the tears on her cheeks reflecting the sunlight.

As we rode I cried, occasionally jerking from a fresh sob.

The social worker's eyes were dry. She turned to me, and in an even, cold voice said: "Stop your crying, Glenn. Mrs. Winston doesn't want you anymore. She doesn't love you."

I looked at her and wondered why she would tell me such a lie. Did she think it would make me feel better or help me adjust sooner to my life's new realities if I could instantly exchange my love for Mother and Father Winston for hate? Instead of believing what she said, I hated her.

We were taken to Pinewood Farms at Marksville, New York—a manicured, sterile dumping ground in the country for kids who had no other place to go. It was to be a temporary home while the agency searched for a more qualified set of foster parents.

For a month or so the Winstons came regularly to see us, always promising that soon we could go home with them again. I knew their address and wrote to them. But then the visits stopped.

Without warning Mother appeared at Christmastime with an armful of presents. I was stunned; Mother usually didn't buy things for us. Stanley and I eagerly grabbed the bright packages, but when we had torn the paper from the last one, I realized something. All of the tags on the gifts were signed, "Love, Mom and Dad Winston."

The "short" stay at Pinewood Farms stretched to eight months, a near eternity for a child separated from the people he loves. I was almost nine and growing hard inside because things always were being taken away from me.

Foster parents were finally found for us. Harold and Fae Brown lived in the quiet White Plains area of the Bronx. They were a young couple—deemed far more suitable than the older Winstons. What the foster care agency didn't know, or chose to ignore, was that Mr. Brown had an alcohol problem, and his wife, worried and angered by his behavior, was emotionally on edge.

My own emotional problems deepened, and before long I was seeing a psychiatrist every Saturday morning. I had many bad habits, like biting my fingernails, stealing, and fighting. Stanley was quiet and cooperative; I was loud and rebellious. I knew I was the most ugly, unlovable, worthless child on earth. While perfecting my self-hate, I learned to hate everybody else too. The psychiatrist wrote in my records, "Glenn is a child who neither loves nor trusts anyone."

The Browns had a baby boy and a four-year-old girl. Mrs. Brown had wanted more children of her own, but a doctor had advised against it. She took in foster kids instead. I guess she loved us, but she was a rigid woman whose punishments were harsh. The way I was behaving, I was punished a lot.

One time she really let me have it. My teeth were full of cavities, so after the dentist started filling them, she ordered me not to buy candy—never, none. This was a tough order for a nine-year-old boy to obey, but I tried.

Mrs. Brown often bought a newspaper at a candy shop near the house, and one day she sent me to buy one. I walked in the candy store, my mouth yearning for a sweet. Before selling me a paper, the shop owner asked me to run an errand for him. When I returned he rewarded me with a chocolate candy bar. Since Mrs. Brown had told me not to *buy* candy and this was a gift, I tore the wrapper off and ate the bar with eager bites.

I arrived home and Mrs. Brown saw chocolate between my teeth. As she grabbed for the leather belt, I blurted out my explanation—my final sentences lapsing into cries for mercy. She whipped me hard, the belt cracking against my skin. Later she sentenced me to go to bed after supper every night for thirty days, with no desserts, no treats, no trips to the movies on Sundays.

Two weeks passed, then a friend invited me to his birthday party. Mrs. Brown said I could go, but she brought me to the party and dramatically announced to the roomful of kids, "Glenn has been a bad boy, so he will not be able to play games or eat cake and ice cream with you."

My friends sat silently for a moment, looking at me as if I were dirty or diseased. I was so embarrassed. My face reddened; I slumped and finally ran from the room crying.

The Browns' marriage was tottering by this time, and they argued and fought frequently. Mr. Brown would come home late at night, a cabbie dropping his wobbly frame at the door. I thought he was sick—I guess he was—but later I learned of his real problem.

The social worker would visit at regular intervals. Stanley and I would say nothing about the storms in the home. We looked at the woman blankly, smiling placidly. "Everything is fine, Ma'am," was our reply to her series of questions. We chose our words carefully. We knew that if necessary the social worker would gladly send us back to Pinewood Farms.

Mother came to visit now and then, and sometimes on the way home from school we would find Mother and Father Winston waiting at a street corner. They still wanted us and rode the subway for miles just to say hello and give us a hug. I learned later that Mrs. Winston was hurt deeply when she lost us—so upset that a doctor had hospitalized her. She overcame her depression only when the doctor convinced her that to be healthy again she would have to let Stanley and me die in her mind.

Mrs. Brown, because of the strains of her crumbling marriage and my own increasingly destructive behavior, finally gave up. She asked the agency to remove us from her home. Our stay had lasted twenty months.

Many of the neighborhood families, and especially the children, seemed sad to see us leave. The Sunday school class and Cub Scout troop Stanley and I had belonged to each gave us a going away party.

I knew Mrs. Brown had been troubled by her own problems. But when I saw the look of pain and sorrow in her face the day we left, I knew she cared. Remembering the sadness in her eyes, from that point on I believed there must be something very evil about me because people could only love me, could only stand me, for a *short* time. I vowed to myself never to get close to anyone again. I was afraid, tired of losing love.

We were taken again to Pinewood Farms, this time to

stay. I cried that first night back. Sure, the Browns had snapped at each other much of the time, and I had felt their anger as the belt slapped against my flesh. But they had given me a home. Now it was gone.

As I whimpered into the night, an older woman at the orphanage took me in her arms and held me. She was Italian, a big-breasted woman who was nearly as wide as she was tall. She stayed there with me until dawn, her compassion and kindness wrapping me like a blanket.

Over and over she whispered as she held me near, "I know it hurts . . . I know it hurts. But there's nothing I can do."

4. Suburb of Hell

Marksville, New York, the 1950s

Seen from the narrow highway that fronted the grounds, Pinewood Farms had a postcard look. A group of dormitories, always agleam with fresh paint, clustered at the bottom of a high but gently sloped hill. The entrance road circled by the edge of a small pond, near which stood the school's administration building. A silver pole towered above its roof, an American flag snapping in the country breeze.

Many of the farms' acres were used for agriculture. Tractors and other farm machines were stored in several barns. On the grounds, in addition to the separate dorms for girls and boys, were a school, gymnasium, swimming pool, athletic fields, and housing for some staff members.

At Pinewood Farms there were no unmowed blades of grass, no gum wrappers in the ditches, no dust particles above door moldings, no grime on kitchen pots. Every plot of sod, every square inch of each building, every piece of equipment was clean and in order.

I'm sure many a woman, passing by in a car with her husband and seeing the flag vivid in the wind, the combed yards, the fresh white buildings, the brightly clothed children at work and play, turned and said, "Oh, it's so clean; what a nice place for those poor children without homes."

It *was* clean and nice on the surface, but on the inside, behind the solid, polished doors, beneath the smiling, washed faces, Pinewood Farms was sick and rotting, a suburb of hell.

It had been November when Mrs. Brown realized she could not handle me any longer and sent Stanley and me to

31

Pinewood. We were now a three-hour drive from New York City. When we arrived we were placed in different housing units. It was official policy to separate family members in this way, an attempt, no doubt, to minimize the rivalry—and loyalty—of brothers and sisters.

I was taken to a "cottage," actually a self-contained section of a large dormitory. There I met my housemother, Mrs. Alice Mitchell, and my eleven roommates. I was ten years old, the youngest boy in the group.

Mrs. Mitchell was a middle-aged, large-boned, fleshy woman. Her graying hair, darkened a shade by oil and perspiration, hung short, barely covering her ears. In her eyes, and in the lines and shadows of her face, I found not a hint of kindness. I learned in time that she was poor, an uneducated widow who had lived a cruel, disappointing life.

The cottage had four single bedrooms and two rooms with four beds each, as well as a bathroom, a small dining area, and a commons room with chairs and a television set. Mrs. Mitchell had a small apartment adjacent to the commons room. She met me at the door, and without pausing to get acquainted, told me the first of many rules: "Glenn, whenever you come in the door, you must take off your shoes."

I could see why. The floors were highly polished and spotless; sunrays, flowing in a side window, bounced brightly from the gleaming surfaces. As we walked toward my room, I saw that every piece of clothing, every chair, every toy or book was in an assigned spot.

In my room Mrs. Mitchell showed me my bed, closet, and dresser drawers. She droned on, explaining in wearing detail how I was to fold socks and underwear, hang shirts and pants, and make the bed military style. I was shown a small drawer where I could store a few personal items. My larger toys had been confiscated when I arrived, placed as communal property in a playroom in the basement.

I learned that two of the older, bigger boys were held responsible for the behavior of the rest of us. Mrs. Mitchell was too old and weak to care for twelve vigorous boys, so she bribed her deputies with cash and privileges and had them solve her problems. If they failed and she heard of some difficulty, she hauled out her cane and whipped them—as well as everybody else. This arrangement was called "the duking system."

I met with the staff psychologist at Pinewood so that he could update my records. I hoped he would send me to someone's home—even a new foster family or back to the Winstons or Browns—but he decided I would be more secure and stable if I remained in an institution indefinitely. His words shattered me; I longed to be far away from the lifeless conformity of Pinewood. I had settled into the routine there, I was being fed and had shelter, but I did not want to stay. I wanted a dad and mom, somebody to talk to, somebody to love.

But the psychologist's decision was final. He had the power to set the course for my life. I don't believe the man's wisdom was ever questioned or his recommendations concerning me and the others ever reviewed—even six months later when he killed himself in his apartment.

So I stayed at Pinewood, and it didn't take me long to learn how to survive at the place. The most important rule was not to show weakness of any kind, particularly crying. At first I saved my tears for late at night. Long after my roommates were asleep, their breathing slow and deep, I would lie awake, lonely, thinking back to my foster homes, the smiling faces and warm hugs. I would hold my emotions as long as I could, but finally my heart would melt and I would cram the pillow over my face and whimper, restraining the sobs and hoping no one would hear. One night, Mrs. Mitchell did hear. She grabbed my shoulders with her heavy hands and shook me, whispering harshly, "Shut up! And don't wake the others."

After a year or so, I hardened. I did not cry anymore, even at night.

December came, and each of us received a holiday gift, two one-dollar bills inside a mimeographed form letter wishing "a Merry Christmas from the Pinewood Farms family." Most of the children left for short visits with relatives or friends. No one, including our mother, came for Stanley and me. The dormitories were nearly empty and achingly quiet. Christmas carols, sounding joyfully from a radio or record player in some distant hall, only reminded me of happier holidays—now seemingly gone forever. Near Christmas Day we had one visitor, Mrs. Brown, and to our surprise she carried with her a nice assortment of wrapped packages. As I read the labels I was stunned; each one was signed, "Love, Mom and Dad Winston." Stanley and I tore the paper from the gifts and had a happy day with our new toys.

The administration at Pinewood believed in a strict, manageable routine. Even before Christmas I had become part of the pattern—meals eaten exactly at the appointed time, school, chores in the dormitory and kitchen, homework, some TV programs, then lights out.

Time was set aside for play, as long as you were on good behavior. I soon learned from the older boys that to amount to anything at Pinewood you had to play adult games—like smoking and messing around with girls. Before my eleventh year ended, I was experienced at both. I pilfered cigarettes from the older boys, and like so many others, met my little girl friends in the woods during recreation periods—the only time other than school and special occasions the sexes were permitted to mingle.

Pinewood was run scientifically and neatly in the most advanced environment social science could offer; but it was still an institutional life incapable of the special treats of a home, like a glass of milk and a cookie at bedtime.

At the cottage we never snacked. There were no vending machines, so if I wanted a candy bar, I had to ask Mrs. Mitchell to draw the money from my account. That spending money came from a weekly allowance, a small reward for dutifully doing the assigned work at the school. Two days later she would bring the coins, and I would buy the candy bar in the kitchen at mealtime. I always ate my

Hershey bar on the spot, stuffing the delicious chocolate into my mouth, afraid some bully would snatch it if I waited.

My main job was in the kitchen. Mrs. Mitchell woke all of us with a whistle at 5:30 A.M. We dressed, made our beds, and cleaned the dormitory. At 6:00 I ran to the school's central kitchen and helped prepare and serve breakfast until 7:30. A half hour later I was in school. At 11:30 I returned to the kitchen, ate hurriedly, then waited on tables in the staff dining room until nearly 1:00 P.M. when school began for the afternoon. In the evening after dinner, I scrubbed pots and pans from 6:00 to 7:30. On Saturday there was more work—five hours cleaning the barns, raking leaves, or picking up trash.

Each week I worked thirty hours for which I was paid fifteen cents.

Other duties continued into the night. As I grew older, Mrs. Mitchell made me get up twice each night to take two boys who were bedwetters to the bathroom. Without an alarm clock, I had trouble at first waking up on time, and the boys wet their sheets. Mrs. Mitchell rapped me with her cane, made me change the bedding, and then ordered me under my bed for two hours. After that I had no trouble waking up since I slept fitfully.

Mrs. Mitchell, with the help of her handpicked deputies, ruled our cottage with an iron fist. Her ways were inconsistent and odd. One minute she could be relaxed, almost kind, purring on in a soothing voice about the love of God and the beauty of Jesus. An instant later, her mood broken by spilled water or a gum wrapper on the floor, she would scream and curse while she thrashed a boy's back with her cane. Her store of patience was low, depleted years ago during the many sad, frustrating days of her life. She must have tried to forget her memories with alcohol. Often, when I emptied the wastebasket in her apartment, I found an empty liquor bottle.

Mrs. Mitchell believed intensely in one of the favorite laws at Pinewood: If you see someone breaking a rule and

you are the first one to report it to a staff member, you will
not be punished. This law destroyed what little unity we
felt and glorified cowardice. In time I trusted no one,
minded my own affairs, and locked my feelings away.

The operators of Pinewood were very sensitive about the
institution's image, and we were warned never to discuss
with visitors or townspeople what went on behind the
gleaming facade. I learned in a painful way how important
that rule was.

Each Sunday a local church hauled a busload of kids
from Pinewood to Sunday school. Mrs. Mitchell, being a
religious woman, herded all of us in her cottage onto the
bus. She went too, clutching in her hand a newspaper that
substituted for her cane when anyone got out of line.

The Sunday school began each week with a large group
meeting. Those of us from Pinewood huddled in our chairs,
stiffly trying to participate in the singing but always
aware that Mrs. Mitchell was behind us—her newspaper
rolled and cocked, ready in an instant to swat down any
too-spirited action on our part.

After the opening session, we divided into smaller
groups by age for a Bible lesson. Here I relaxed, finally out
of sight of my eagle-eyed housemother. Mrs. Mitchell had
warned us to be nice and sociable but not to get too chum-
my with any outsider. But in my class was a boy named
Terry. We liked each other and became friends.

One Sunday after class, Terry's parents walked up.
"Glenn, would you like to come home with us for dinner
today?" Terry's mother asked.

I wanted to go so much, but I was scared. I didn't say
anything, then looked longingly at Mrs. Mitchell, who was
standing nearby, listening.

"Would it be all right if I had lunch with these people?" I
asked her.

She smiled sweetly. "Sure, no problem. Go ahead and
have a good time." Her response bothered me vaguely, but
bubbling with excitement, I happily went on my way.

That Sunday afternoon was probably normal for Terry

and his family, but for me it was a holiday, each minute a savored taste of freedom. The house was full of relatives. We ate a large meal, all of us grouped closely around a long table. I was not singled out for special attention and was allowed to relax and be myself.

Later in the afternoon, I shared a few things about my past. Terry's parents sat beside me a moment, and before driving me to Pinewood, they prayed for me and my problems.

I arrived back at the cottage at 6:30 P.M. As I climbed the stairway I noted something unusual: It was absolutely quiet. Since the main dining room was closed on Sunday evenings, usually at this time the boys were in the commons room, laughing, preparing sandwiches and opening soft drinks, waiting to watch *Walt Disney* on television. Tonight there was no sound of clanking dishes or potato chip packages being ripped open.

When I entered the living room I saw that every one of my cottage mates was standing motionless, facing a corner or a wall. Off in the side room I could hear sounds coming from Mrs. Mitchell's TV set. I said rather meekly, "I'm back."

"Get in here," Mrs. Mitchell yelled. I walked in and she threw me to the floor and kicked me in the back.

"You dirty son of the devil," she cried. "I told you not to get close to those people. Just because of you, nobody here had any dinner, and they've been standing out there since church while you were having a good time."

The woman stood over me, her lips snarled, the hate boiling in her eyes. I was terrified, sick in my stomach.

Mrs. Mitchell dragged me into the commons room. She had the eleven others each get a stick or paddle and lined them up in a row. Each boy spread his legs, and as I crawled through on my hands and knees, he smashed my buttocks as hard as he could. Near the end of the line I had to clamp my jaws to keep from crying out in pain after each blow.

When the ritual was over, I was made to approach each

boy, speak his name, and apologize. Every one of them then slapped my face. Mrs. Mitchell lectured me some more and warned me not to let it happen again.

My face ached, and I could feel small blood spots forming and drying on the back of my underwear. I went to my room and laid myself carefully on the bed. I stared at the ceiling, dazed and confused. But I didn't cry. The soft spot I once had inside was gone, buried under a surging flood of hate.

5. The Little Boy Is Dead

Marksville, New York, the 1960s

"You gotta earn your keep around here. I don't accept weaklings. Weaklings are not permitted."

His favorite lines spoken, John Williams, the man who ran Pinewood Farms, walked away, slapping a short, wood switch against his thigh.

Several of us watched him go, swearing at him in low tones. We had been cutting weeds with hand scythes beside a road before he showed up to whip us with his tongue. As he had stood there, using his condemning glare to prod us into productivity, I had bitten my cheek to keep from laughing at his ridiculous appearance. He was not short, but his squarish head topped with a bushy crewcut, rounded shoulders, and billowing stomach made him look dwarfish.

My recollection of Williams during my early months at Pinewood is hazy. But as I grew older and more rebellious, he and I tangled more often. I despised the man and vowed that when I grew up I would hunt him down and kill him.

This hot August morning, not long after Williams left, I felt blisters rising on my hands. I had been cutting with the scythe for three hours, and the pain made it hard to curl my fingers and grip the handle. I dropped the tool and walked to the first aid room.

The nurse looked at my puffy, red hands, but seemed insulted at having to treat such a minor complaint. We were never to visit her unless deathly ill or bleeding profusely. A middle-aged, brusque woman, she had been a nurse at Pinewood for some time. Most of her days were spent driving kids to town for doctor visits, a task which required her to be a combination chauffeur/drill sergeant. I think she hated her work but was trapped in the job by uncontrollable circumstances.

"Come here," the nurse ordered, grabbing my hands and pulling me toward the medicine cabinet. To my horror she reached for a dark bottle and dabbed the sores generously with iodine. The brown liquid seared my nerve endings, and I yelped in pain, pulling my hands away from her.

"Now, go out there and work," the nurse said after I calmed down.

"But my hands are like raw meat," I replied.

"Go out and work, you lazy no-good," she said more firmly, her voice rising. My hands throbbing and sore, I returned to cutting weeds.

Except for our allowance, we were never paid for any of the work, even when people in the area or friends of staff members would borrow us on Saturday for ten hours of window washing or lawn mowing. Pinewood called these efforts "earning your keep."

"You should be grateful to God that he has blessed you with a place like Pinewood," Williams often would say. "You could be out on the street starving." He was right, I suppose, although I learned years later that the state of New York paid most of the bills for the care of the kids at the orphanage. "Earning our keep" could better have been described as "slavery."

Williams ran Pinewood as though it were a military boot camp. We were always in training—plenty of running, pushups, and other exercises. And in true military fashion, our living quarters were inspected.

Every two weeks on Saturday afternoon, Mr. Williams would stalk into the cottage, bearing himself like a proud colonel, his fat hands stuffed in white gloves. Each of us stood at attention by our beds. Every closet door was open, all shirts and pants hung exactly in the prescribed manner. The dresser drawers were pulled out, the underwear and socks folded and placed precisely. Williams would glide his white-gloved hand across chairs, bed railings, and dresser tops. If he found a speck of dust he would shriek, "You slobs! How can you live in a pigpen like this?"

There was a need to keep our rooms clean and in order, but Williams seemed obsessed with mindless regimentation. The bed gave me the most trouble; we were required to make it with hospital corners, pulling the sheets and blanket drum-tight. Mr. Williams carried a ruler and would measure the corners on the blanket. Then he would bounce a quarter on the taut covering. If the coin didn't spring back satisfactorily, he would yell: "Hester! When are you going to learn how to make a bed?" I would cringe. Whenever anyone in the cottage failed inspection, everyone was made to work extra hours.

There was one group of kids at Pinewood who didn't work—athletes. Mr. Williams loved sports, and he expected our school to excel in all athletic events. I didn't care much for sports. Although I was twelve years old and as tall as the other boys my age, I remained skinny, weak, and uncoordinated. My poor physical stamina and abilities, not to mention my rebellious loner temperament, made me a poor candidate for Pinewood's teams. My nearest involvement with athletics came when I picked rocks on the ball fields.

All of us nonjocks were expected to serve as personal valets to the athletes. Not only were the athletes excused from chores, but unknown to the administration, they rarely did their own schoolwork. Several athletes lived in my cottage, and they forced me to do their homework. Each night I would work their math problems and other assignments. This was a sophisticated scheme; not only did I do the work, but I also learned to copy exactly each boy's handwriting. My own homework had to be done, too, though the athletes forced me to make many errors on my own papers. I was doing schoolwork for four people, yet failing some classes myself.

I don't think the teachers ever figured the system out. They always wondered why the athletes got A's on homework but flunked tests. I passed tests easily, but my homework scores were low. School became just another bitter joke to me.

One morning in Mrs. Thompson's geography class, George Miller, one of Pinewood's notorious bullies, passed me a note from his desk three spots behind me. It read, "Mrs. Thompson is a real bitch."

I wadded up the paper and threw it back at George. With an innocent expression masking his face, he stood up and said: "Mrs. Thompson, excuse me. Look what Glenn gave me."

The lady read the note, looked darkly at me, and then hustled me to the principal's office. There I was ordered to not just drop my pants but to remove them completely. The principal unrolled the leather belt he kept coiled in a desk drawer.

"Bend over that desk, you foul-mouthed animal," the man yelled as he slashed the doubled belt across my backside. Between swings I tried to protest and explain, but the beating went on.

When it was over, I slowly stood erect and pulled on my trousers. I could feel the blood blisters forming. I knew from experience that sitting down would be nearly impossible for days. I walked from the office, saying nothing, leaving the principal wiping the belt with a rag.

Since I no longer cried to relieve my hurts, I concentrated on getting even. Revenge became my only sweet satisfaction in life. Two weekends after being beaten by the principal, I broke into a school room and knocked everything—every book, picture, and flower pot—to the floor. I wasn't strong enough yet to hurt people with my fists, but I found ways to scratch back at those who wronged me. Instead of crying and pouting, I dumped sugar into gas tanks or slashed tires.

After Mrs. Brown's early visits with Stanley and me ended and we lost contact with the outside world, I tried writing letters for a while. About once every two months I would scrawl out a bit of news and mention the usual gripes and send the note to the Winstons or Browns. I always wrote about the brutality at the farms and begged them to come get me. I had no money for stamps, but the staff at Pinewood promised to mail two letters a week without charge. I dropped the letters in a box on the grounds, but no letters from the outside ever were delivered to me. I wondered why Mrs. Winston or Mrs. Brown didn't write back; at the time I thought it was because they didn't care. Years later I learned they had wondered the same thing about me. For reasons I'll probably never know, something happened to my mail at Pinewood.

Almost two years passed at the farms before Mother stopped by for a visit—smiling, ready once again to try her hand at motherhood. She had a new common-law husband, Tom, and for once I liked her man. He was a plumber, a decent, level-headed fellow. Mother came regularly for almost two months, and even took Stanley and me home for Thanksgiving.

During that visit, a woman living in an apartment two floors above Mother's asked me to come and help her carry out some trash bags. She was about thirty years old and lived alone. I knocked on her door, and she asked me in and gave me some cookies. It became obvious in only a few minutes that she had plans for me other than hauling garbage. She removed her clothing, helped me take off mine, and led me to her bedroom where we had intercourse. I was frightened, afraid the woman would tell someone what had happened and get me into trouble. I said not a word to anyone. I was twelve years old.

After we had been back at Pinewood a few weeks, Mother's visits dropped off. Months would pass, and then she would appear—her face always bearing a blank, guiltless look, as though she had just been away from us long enough to shake a rug. I no longer desired her love and often wished she would go away for good.

My teen years began, and when I examined my chest and arms in a mirror, I realized I no longer was skinny and weak. The work in the fields had hardened my body. I began to test my strength, challenging the bullies and get-

ting even with others by using my fists. The violence
worsened with each round of revenge, and there was no
escaping the tension and anxiety that filled each day and
night. I did not attempt to share this burden by forming
close friendships. I wanted to avoid the additional hurt of
relying on others, only to have them fail me. I was still
afraid, but almost daily had to prove that I was tough and
had no weakness. I fought and fought, catching fury from
all sides.

One night long after midnight, I was sleeping with my
head half submerged in a pillow, facing the center of the
room. Suddenly I felt a wet, sticky material being ground
against my mouth and face. Struggling to shake myself
from the blackness of sleep, I smelled what it was too late. I
leaped up, cursing and swinging my fists, but my tormen-
tor fled. All I could do was rush to the bathroom and scrub
the human excrement from my face.

But I, too, loved the safety of darkness for carrying out
my revenge. Once in the middle of the night I took a cast
iron frying pan I had sneaked from the kitchen and glided
softly to Steve Wilson's bed. I don't recall what he had done
to deserve his punishment, but it was my move in our
brutal game. As he lay peacefully, I raised the heavy pan
high and smashed it with all my force into his face. I was
out of the room before he raised a cry, the blood spurting
from his horribly crushed nose.

I'm not proud of the way I hurt Steve and the others;
after I had hurt someone, I would ask myself, "Why are you
doing this?" I was twisted, cold, and angry inside. I wanted
love and attention, somebody to put an arm around my
shoulder and find some good in me. But it never happened,
so I forced people to notice me by letting my boiling hate
and fury blow out like a volcano, crushing and burning
those who offended and hurt me.

Once in a while my revenge resembled justice, like the
time Mike Porter, a boy I liked, broke a toilet seat. The
bathrooms at Pinewood had institutional toilets, plain
white fixtures topped with coverless wooden seats. Toilet

seats were a grave issue at Pinewood. Williams and the housemothers spoke often about the dire punishments awaiting boys who urinated without lifting the seat. In fact, one boy in my cottage committed this sin one day, and having left some wet evidence, was caught by Mrs. Mitchell. I don't think he did it again, not after he wiped up his mistake with his face.

One day my friend Mike dropped a toilet seat down and it split and a piece broke off. The seat was old, ready to be replaced anyway, but the housemother showed no mercy and made Mike buy a new one with his allowance money. Since we were given fifteen cents a week, he lost a year's pay.

I decided this housemother needed a lesson. One afternoon my opportunity came. The lady left her purse in a room, and I darted in and stole two twenty-dollar bills. I quickly slipped them into my shoe just before the housemother returned. She was immediately suspicious and checked her billfold. I was the only potential criminal in the vicinity, so I became the prime suspect. Mr. Williams was called, and while he conducted the investigation, I was placed in his car. During the early moments of confusion, I slipped the money from my shoe and stuck it behind the seat.

Williams came back, dragged me from the car, and searched me. "Where is that money, you swine?" he yelled, shaking me by the shoulders, the movement jerking his bare, balloonlike belly out from beneath his shirt.

"I don't know nothin' about no money, Mr. Williams," I replied innocently. He slapped me a few times with his switch and pushed me against the car, but I didn't confess. The housemother and others searched the room carefully but couldn't find the money. Every time the incident came to mind, I laughed about it.

Six months later when Williams was cleaning out his car, he lifted the seat and saw the bills. I got it good, a whipping and ten hours of extra work.

There were a few breaks in my escalating misery at

Pinewood. I didn't do it often, but sometimes I would lie on my bed and read the Bible Mrs. Brown had bought me when I lived at her house. I liked Psalm 100, "Make a joyful noise to the Lord. . . . It is he that made us . . . we are his people, and the sheep of his pasture."

One day I was flipping through the Old Testament and I read that God would punish children for the sins of their fathers. This made me mad. Why should God make me suffer for the useless life of my father? From that day on I didn't take time for God and religion. I wanted to get my hands on God and strangle him for sticking me with such a rotten life.

In the summertime, if we were not doing extra work for disciplinary reasons, the staff freed us for recreation in the afternoon. Since I hated team sports, I would go fishing by myself at a quiet spot on a nearby river. I enjoyed these few hours of peace, a brief retreat from the fear and violence.

Once a month Pinewood would bus us to a movie theater in Marksville. We were a traveling exhibition of "boys gone bad." At the movie house we marched in single file through a side door and sat together, all wearing the same kind of cheaply cut shirts and pants, our hair short and shaped by the farms' barber in the same mold. If any boy laughed too loudly or got overly excited, a housemother in the row behind would tap him on the head with a ruler. When the movie was over, we left through the side exit, isolated like lepers. This outing always shamed me, and I was almost relieved and glad to arrive back at the combed, sparkling compound.

My fourteenth birthday came. I didn't know it, but my days at Pinewood were nearing an end. The violence swirling inside me like a tornado was becoming more than Williams and his cohorts could stomach.

One night I was walking down a hallway when three boys jumped me and pulled me into a shower room. I fought, straining to pull away, but they wrestled me to the floor. While two of them held me, the third unbuckled my belt and pulled my trousers and underwear to my ankles.

As I kicked and swore, he stepped back and grabbed a BB gun, cocked it, and fired the shot point-blank into my testicles.

I fell limp, no longer needing to be subdued. Before they ran, the three of them stood over me, watching to see if I would break down, maybe even cry. The pain sickened me, and I nearly blacked out. After the boys left I groaned; my body glistened from a fine film of sweat, but I saw no blood. I dressed and limped back to my bed, fearing I would vomit. I didn't cry.

It took a few weeks, but I caught each of these boys alone. As I beat them unmercifully, I suppressed my fear of what they might do to me next.

Mother started visiting again, and I was now so inwardly afraid and anxious to leave that I begged her to take me home. She refused, so I stepped up my terrorism, hoping Pinewood's administrators would be forced to get rid of me. I also ran away as often as I could, one time making it to Washington, D. C. I wandered around in the capital city for two days before I got hungry and turned myself in. The police shipped me back. My strategy worked. Pinewood summoned Mother and said that either she must take me home or I would be sent to a reform school.

A week before I left, a staff worker at the farms caught me alone in a storage shed. We had not gotten along; I think he wanted to spill some of his anger on me while he had a chance.

"You're nothing but a troublemaker, Hester," he said, and then he punched me twice in the head with both fists, the second blow smashing against my ear. I was dazed and struggled to keep on my feet. My ear rang loudly, and when I touched it blood spotted my hand.

I walked to the nurse's office and told her what had happened. She was having another in her long string of miserable days.

"You dirty liar," she cried and slapped my face. Shaking with anger she poured some olive oil in the ear and plugged it with cotton.

"Get out of here," she said, pointing to the door.

I walked out, bells ringing in my ear. The noise clamoring in that ear didn't stop, and my hearing has never fully recovered.

My departure date came in mid-May. A social worker drove out from the city to pick Stanley and me up. I waited for her, my unfolded clothes dumped in two shopping bags. Four years of my life were gone. The little boy I had been, the one who had cried through that first night at Pinewood—longing for the warmth of somebody's arms—was dead. In his place was a surly, broken teen-ager, one who never cried, who no longer dreamed of love, but instead lived for revenge.

As the social worker drove slowly out the drive, pulling away from the administration building with its flag flapping gloriously in the breeze, I asked her to stop the car just before we reached the highway. I opened the door, stood, and looked back, seeing for the last time the white buildings, the pond, the clipped bushes, the boys picking stones in the fields. I clenched my fists. "One day I'll get even with all of you. May this place go to hell!" I yelled and spat on the ground.

In the distant field a boy raised his head and looked my way for a moment. Then without a sign he stooped and went back to work. I stepped in the car and stared straight ahead as we drove away.

6. I Want Someone to Love Me

Manhattan, the 1960s

I was home at last, free from the miseries of Pinewood. But my problems were not so easily left behind; they settled in with me in New York City as I tried again to be part of a family.

Mother and I could not get along, our wills scraping against each other like coarse sandpaper. Four years had passed, and I no longer knew how to function in the fragile environment of family life. I talked back belligerently and always balked at parental orders—especially those dumped by the carload on me by Mother. I hated her and didn't know how to forgive. I blamed her for my pain. Living with her, I sought ways to make her hurt too.

I relished, though, my new freedom and small measure of peace. Mother and Tom lived in an aging but clean and sturdy apartment building on West 166th Street in Manhattan. The two were building supervisors, and the family was squeezed into the "super's" basement quarters. In addition to Stanley and me, that included a younger sister and brother, Linda and Steve.

Mother was a tidy housekeeper. The faded, worn-smooth pieces of furniture rested precisely in the tiny rooms. Dust was collected regularly, and trash went out daily. The kids were commanded to keep clothes and belongings picked up. After my four years of enforced tidiness, I longed to be sloppy—and was most of the time, a festering irritation between Mother and me.

The apartment building was succumbing to old age, and we all worked hard to keep its decay contained. Our first month at home, Stanley and I painted woodwork and hallways and shoveled coal into an aging boiler used for heating the building's hot water. This maintenance work could have lasted all summer—there was much to do—but it meant Mother and I were in striking distance twenty-four hours a day. We used the time effectively, sharpening the edges of our cutting tongues on each other.

When I would run my mouth too far, Mother would give me a shove or slap me. Sometimes I pushed back, and often I wanted to hit her. Tom saw the danger signs, and to get me away from Mother he began taking me to work with him.

I liked Tom very much. By trade he was a plumber, but he was skillful at carpentry and auto mechanics, too. I admired how he gracefully handled the tools with his large, toughened hands. I wanted to be like him. I worked beside him, copying and learning his movements. I was a young, mouthy punk, but Tom quietly accepted me, showing deep reserves of patience. If my turbulent ways bothered him, he didn't show it.

For several weeks we rode the subway together to Brooklyn where Tom worked. At first I carried his tools and hauled pipe. Later Tom showed me how the wrenches worked, and I became his helper. The adult setting suited me. I enjoyed being able to smoke cigarettes when I wanted to, and I was elated to be away from Mother's whining. This arrangement ended abruptly when Tom's boss learned I was only fourteen years old. Having me at work violated a child labor law, so Tom was told to leave me at home.

Together again around the clock, Mother and I picked up our battle. Our relationship bottomed out. Rightfully so, Mother did not trust me. She lived in fear, noting how my strength had ripened.

One Sunday morning Tom wanted a newspaper. Sitting on the living room couch, he opened his wallet and found only a five-dollar bill. He handed it to me, and I was almost out the door when Mother stopped me.

"Glenn, where are you going with that money?" she asked suspiciously.

"I'm goin' to get a paper for Tom—he told me to," I said and turned to leave.

"Give that money here," Mother snapped. She grabbed the bill from my hand and marched into Tom.

"Don't give Glenn this much money," she scolded. "He won't bring any change back."

I yelled a curse at her, then slammed the door as I left. I wanted to run away but had no money and wasn't sure where I would go. So I went back.

One night in late June, I picked a fight with Stanley. We were pushing each other noisily, knocking aside furniture in the living room, working each other over pretty good.

"Stop it, Glenn," Mother ordered, rushing in from the kitchen.

"Mind your own business," I answered angrily, stepping again toward Stanley. Before I reached him, Mother grabbed me from behind, swung me around, and slapped my face. I reacted instantly, slapping her so hard she yelped and ducked away.

"You do that again, and I'll kill you," I screamed at her.

Mother said nothing more, just rubbed her jaw and walked to the telephone. She called the police, telling them to come and arrest me.

Two officers came. Mother cried a bit as she told them I was incorrigible and beyond her control. Later, the probation officer investigating my case realized the situation at home could only get worse—somebody would get badly hurt. He recommended I be placed somewhere else.

I went before a judge. Not certain what to do with me, the judge sent me to Spofford, New York City's Youth House or holding facility for teen-age criminals.

Spofford, a four-story, gray stone building covering an entire block in the Bronx, was supposed to be a haven for juvenile offenders, a place where teen-agers in trouble could be evaluated and helped. In fact, it was a prison, a finishing school for vicious punks wanting to refine their techniques of crime and violence.

I was not an innocent weakling, but in my first hours at Spofford I realized I was still a rookie at being mean and brutal. I entered Spofford at the time when New York's street gangs were rampant. The place bulged, filled with hundreds of muggers, rapists, killers, and others like myself. Most of these boys lived without hope, knowing that when they left Spofford no job or golden American suburban dream awaited them. Most of them were poor, semi-literate, alone. Spofford seethed with adolescent tension, violence erupting at whim day after day.

My clothes were taken, and I was given a uniform—blue denim pants and shirt. I was assigned a private room with a door that could be locked or unlocked only from the outside. I slept there, but spent most of my time elsewhere. At night we were made to strip off our denims and underwear, leaving them folded in a pile in the hallway. We crept naked into our barren cells. Each of these rooms had a small window covered with heavy wire mesh. Escape was impossible. The rooms were on the fourth floor, and even with two bedsheets tied together, the drop to the street was three stories. Anyway, the idea of escaping nude was bad enough by itself to stop most of us.

Every day started early. At 5:00 A.M. an attendant banged on each door and blew a whistle. We made our beds and then stumbled in groups of ten to the showers. Then we put on our denims, swept the floors, and lined up for breakfast.

By 6:00 A.M. we were standing at attention, ready to eat. No talking was allowed in line. Hundreds of us stood wordlessly in the long, neon-lit halls. The only sound, other than the whistles and curses of the guards, was the rumble of hundreds of stamping feet. To keep us from mischief, the guards made us march in place, endlessly it seemed, until the command was given to head for the dining room.

Most of us could not keep our mouths shut while in line. We would whisper to the guy in front. Sometimes a guard, one of many thick-necked, cloudy-eyed musclemen, would sidle quietly up from the rear and catch a whisper. A black boot would smash into your rear, sprawling you on the floor. To the end of the line you went, maybe one hundred and fifty places back.

At the entrance to the dining hall, we were handed a metal tray, spoon, and rounded knife. Forks, thought to be too deadly a potential weapon, were not distributed. We could talk during the meal but had to gobble the food in just ten minutes. When done, a guard checked in our tray and silverware. At the exit we were searched, made to drop our pants and underwear, bend over, and spread our "cheeks"—a demeaning ritual supposedly performed to prevent smuggling of anything that could be made into a weapon. No doubt the many homosexuals on the staff found this harassment inspiring.

On weekday mornings we attended a school operated within Spofford. I was enrolled in the eighth grade, but third-grade material was being taught. Under these circumstances I was considered a brilliant student. Many of my peers couldn't read and dozed off in class.

School ended at lunchtime, and the afternoon provided some variety. We could swim in the pool or shoot baskets in the gymnasium. Boxing was a favorite diversion. The guards loved boxing; many of them were ex-fighters. If a teen-aged inmate had a disagreement with a guard, the boy would be invited into the ring by the guard to resolve the problem. Most of the guards were big and strong and mauled the weaker, less experienced boys. I weighed 135 pounds and avoided such boxing matches at all costs.

About one month after I went to Spofford, at 11:00 in the evening I was in my room nearly asleep. A key clicked into the lock on my door, the latch turned, and a guard—a muscular, dark haired man—glided into the room. Softly, he removed the key and closed the door behind him. I scrambled to my feet and backed against the far wall, my pulse jumping. The man stepped to within two feet of me and stopped.

"You sure are a nice lookin' little boy, Hester," the man whispered, his teeth glinting from the neon light that burned all night.

I knew what he wanted. I had seen that lust in a man's eyes before. I stood motionless, half crouching, trying to cover my nakedness by twisting my body sideways. I was helpless; we both knew it. If I yelled he would bust open my skull. The guard carried a billy club in his right hand. He reached out with the stick and placed it behind my back, penning me in. His left hand came toward me. It was calloused, and on the back several twisted blood vessels pulsed just below the skin. The left hand touched my stomach, covered it, and then slid slowly down. I jumped; his hand was cold. Bubbling with fear and anger, my adrenalin rising, I was about to strike him when a noise sounded down the hall—a slamming door, someone crying out in his sleep, I don't know what it was. Without a word, the man turned and left, locking the door smoothly behind him. I slumped back on the bed, shaking.

My stay at Spofford stretched on. About every six weeks I would be brought, handcuffed to a long chain with several others, before the judge of family court. He always asked me the same question.

"Glenn Hester: What do you want for your life?"

"I want a family, someone to love me."

A Spofford staff member would present a report. The judge would then request more tests and evaluation. I would be handcuffed and led back to Spofford.

My "psychological testing and evaluation" there took place in a large group setting. A moronic guard would pace in front of about fifty of us. His approach was simple and direct.

"Has any of you got any problems or something to say?" he would yell.

"No, sir!" we would answer, shouting in chorus. With that our therapy session ended for another week, and we marched stiffly from the room.

No one at Spofford seemed to like me. I was a little,

smart-mouthed, blue-eyed white kid in a place where eight of ten inmates and staff were black or Hispanic. And it didn't take long before everyone found out I was at Spofford for hitting my mother. About the only human being on earth these killers and rapists respected was their own mommy; they didn't care for someone who had roughed up his mother.

I was forced to fight constantly, losing about as often as I won. Everyday at Spofford I saw blood—pools of it—on the floor. Sometimes, while walking up a stairway, someone coming down the steps would stick out a foot and trip me, just to start a rumble. I would hit the guy as hard as I could. Instantly, all the boys on the stairway would start swinging, slashing away at the nearest body in sight. The guards would run up with their clubs and beat us down.

I learned it was unwise to end up cut badly or to get knocked unconscious. If your injury was too serious, the staff had to send you to a hospital. When you returned from being treated, two or three guards would corner you and start shoving.

"Did you say anything to somebody at the hospital, Hester?" they would yell. The guards always feared some outsider might accuse them of using unnecessary force.

"Hester, you said something, what did you say?" I didn't answer. After a while they tired of bumping you against a wall.

The guards scared me some, but the other teen-agers caused the real terror. They were like caged, hungry, wild animals, and I was small and looked vulnerable. Many of them carried weapons—no guns or knives, just small pieces of glass or sharp bits of metal. Some boys taped remnants of a razor blade between their fingers. If an opponent was armed this way, his simple slap would slice half of your face into ribbons.

Many mornings when I awakened, my entire body ached from the previous day's fighting. I couldn't win every time, but I made certain I hurt each one I brawled with—a busted tooth, a bitten ear, a deep scratch on the cheek.

They tried to do the same to me: One day some boy's fist found my mouth and chipped my front tooth.

The guards encouraged us to settle problems with fist fights. A favorite staff amusement was to stage a fight between two kids who were not getting along. The spectators, guards included, would bet cigarettes (we had no money) on who would win. I became convinced that problems in life could only be solved by violence and physical power.

While at Spofford, like most everyone, I exercised to strengthen myself. In my cell before I went to sleep, I did pushups and deep knee-bends by the hundreds.

Six months passed. I wondered how long my "temporary" stay at Spofford would last. I did want to stay long enough to settle one more score—and thought about this revenge constantly. I had not forgotten that guard and his late night visit. Each day I searched for a moment when I could repay him, but it seemed the opportunity would never come. No one knew what he had tried to do to me. I feared if the word got out, someone else might think I welcomed those late night visitors. I kept my hate simmering and waited.

My chance came one afternoon when a group of us were playing cards in the lounge. The guard was in the room, lazily watching us, tapping his club on his knee. He turned his back for an instant to pick up a piece of paper he had dropped behind him. I leaped, grabbed a wooden chair, raised it above his head, and smashed it down on his skull. He screamed in pain. I climbed on his back, clenched his neck with my free hand, and smashed his face repeatedly with the other fist.

The man shook his mammoth head, trying to clear his brain. Finally he toppled to the floor, and the others in the room leaped on him like vultures, kicking him and smashing his body with chairs and ashtrays. Another guard ran into an adjoining office, locked the door, and hit an emergency alarm. In a minute, a dozen guards stormed in, knocking my snarling friends and me down with clubs. We were dragged away and locked up.

Two days later I was declared insane. The staff at Spofford told the judge I was dangerous and might kill someone. Those reports were probably true.

I never had a chance to tell the judge my side of the story, about that late night visit. I had learned sometime ago I had to make my own justice in the world.

7. Oh Baby, I'ma Nuts Over You

Manhattan, the 1960s

The guards at Spofford never had a chance to beat me after I gave their coworker his headache. They wanted to, I'm sure, but I was scheduled to see the judge a few days after the attack. The guards couldn't risk having me limp into court, covered with scars and bruises.

The judge determined my problems were in my head and ordered me transferred to a psychiatric hospital. The morning I left Spofford, two guards took me aside. One of them grunted, "Don't say nothin' to anybody about what happened here. You do, and we'll come and get you."

I believed them.

The New York State Psychiatric Institute on Fort Washington Street in Manhattan was affiliated with Columbia University. The judge did me a favor sending me there; the institute was a progressive hospital, staffed with competent professionals who wanted to help me. Ultimately they failed, but it wasn't because the doctors and nurses didn't try.

On a cool, gray, mid-November day, I was hauled in a police van across town, over the Harlem River to upper Manhattan. During the ride my hands were cuffed to a thick steel bar, but when the van halted at the institute's door, the handcuffs were opened. I stepped out, appearing to be just another acne-faced teen-ager stopping by for a visit—not a violent criminal.

The institute, housed in Columbia's Presbyterian Medical Center, was located in a twenty-story building that stradled a cliff. An attendant rode the elevator with me to the administrative offices on the tenth floor. Mother was waiting. I asked her about Tom and my brothers and sister. She hurriedly answered, "They're fine," and then began to scold me for being in more trouble. I stared at a spot high on the wall behind her, refusing to pay attention.

A woman wearing a white coat entered, then led us to an office for an interview. I told my story once more, revealing only the bare outline of my troubled past. I did not trust the lady interviewer. Foolishly, I feared she would tell my keepers at Spofford if I said anything bad about them. I thought no one would believe what a punk kid had to say anyway.

Mother signed the commitment papers; I was now officially a mental patient, eligible for shock treatments, drugs, and all the other "advanced" techniques used to unscramble a twisted life like mine. I knew I had problems, but I didn't think I was crazy. I wondered what they would do to me, and I was scared.

The interview ended and Mother left. Another white-clothed attendant took me on the elevator down to the sixth floor. We were met there by an orderly, a tall, robust black man also wearing crisp whites. He walked toward me briskly, and I cowered, half expecting him to slap or push me. Spofford was fresh in mind, and I still expected violence to erupt at any time.

"Take it easy, man," the orderly said, his words ending in a deep-voiced chuckle. "Nobody's goin' to hit you." I relaxed some.

The orderly told me I must take a shower. He pointed toward a bathroom.

"Aren't you comin'?" I asked. At Spofford we never took a shower alone.

"Why, you want me to hold your hand?" he answered, laughing again. Maybe this place wouldn't be as bad as I had feared.

"How much time can I have in the shower?" I asked.

"How much time you want, man?" he replied.

Such a luxury shocked me—a private, drawn-out shower. In the shower room I found normal bath soap, not the lye-filled, hard bars provided at Spofford. I stood under the warm, cleansing stream for ten minutes.

As I finished toweling off, the orderly brought me fresh clothing—a colorful sport shirt and a dark pair of casual slacks.

"You allow people to wear this kind of clothes?" I asked, thinking of the Spofford denims. This time the orderly just shook his head before he laughed.

Soon after I dressed, dinner was served—not in a mess hall, but in a bright, cheerful dining area. Long tables were already set with dishes and silverware, even forks. There were forty men in the ward, and except for several patients who had been chosen to serve, the rest of us took our places. I was speechless, expecting any moment to wake from a dream back in my cell at Spofford. As dishes of food were passed, a patient, acting as waiter, poured water into my glass. As I sipped—finding myself a bit self-conscious about table manners—I remembered it had been six months since my last drink from anything but a tin cup at a meal.

I asked my table mates how many minutes we had to eat. They stared at me quizzically. Donny, an overweight six-teen-year-old, said haughtily, "We finish dinner here when we feel like it."

I looked around. No guards were screaming curses or pushing people against the walls. The scene seemed more like a banquet than dinner hour at a mental hospital.

After the meal I sat down in a lounge chair to smoke a cigarette. I divided my gaze between a television set and the other patients. The men varied in age, and I saw about six others who appeared to be teen-agers. The mood was relaxed. The patients, orderlies, and nurses moved calmly through the rooms, exchanging small talk, smoking cigarettes, drinking coffee. No one acted crazy; I began to unwind.

The evening slipped by. At 10:30 I was quite tired and asked a nurse where my cell was. She laughed, then walked me to a large open room with twenty beds. She assigned one to me, and after she left, I undressed and crawled in. At 11:00 the lights were turned off. Sinking into sleep, I realized I had not slept where no light glared all night since leaving home the previous summer.

After a few days I was certain the institute was a better place than Spofford, but I still trusted no one. My interviews continued, and in each I sparred with my questioner, revealing only what bits of information I felt could be surrendered without risking more punishment. Staff members at the institute strained to understand and help me, but I was too far gone, too old, too twisted by my own insecurity and fears. If I had been less explosive by nature, I might have survived long enough at the institute to regain emotional stability and be released. But I was burned out mentally. I hated all authority and could never give in to rules for long. The institute had many rules; I began to break them one by one.

The rule concerning student nurses caused me the most trouble. A patient was never to touch a nurse—in particular the young female students who put in six weeks of psychiatric on-the-job training in our ward. But I wanted to touch those nurses real bad.

When I came to the institute I was only fourteen, but my attitudes made me feel much older. I knew all about sex, having educated myself in the woods with my girl friends at Pinewood. I had been sexually active since age eleven and had the moral outlook of an alley tomcat. I was in the heart of my hot adolescence, and I thought of sex constantly. Many of the student nurses were only nineteen, a bit naive, just a year or two away from conservative homes in the Midwest or elsewhere. I had a high opinion of my romantic prowess, and the sight of these young nurses, clean and crisp in their sparkling white uniforms, tormented me day and night.

My "romantic moves" actually were clumsy, but at the time I thought I was clever and subtle. I would pick out an appealing student nurse—one who was new to our ward—walk up to her, and wrap my arm tenderly around her shoulder.

"How are you, sweetheart," I would ask invitingly, a wide smile lighting my pimpled face.

"Oh, oh, just fine," the girl would answer, the fear sounding in her voice and flickering around the outer corners of her smile. She would awkwardly duck and pull away.

After all, this is a hospital for deranged people. I could almost see the thought darting through her mind. I loved this initial reaction, the fear I saw in the eyes.

Although I thought I was Cassanova, to the nurses my behavior must have been crude and ludicrous. One of my favorite lines was, "Do you want to slip under the sheets with me?" That one always brought me trouble and was never even remotely successful. I thought this was enormously humorous, me offering the whole marital experience to some quivering, ninety-five-pound girl fresh from the sticks. I frightened many of them, my eyes glazed, reddened, and wild from the drugs.

Most of the patients received medication. A nurse, wheeling a shiny steel cart covered with small white cups, each containing one or more pills, came by at least twice a day. The doctor had me on Thorazine and other drugs. The first time I received my medicine cup, I noticed the Thorazine tablets were identical to the "vitamins" I and some other rowdy boys had been given at Pinewood.

When I used Thorazine my mind was alert, but I could not make my body move quickly. I always had to concentrate a moment on what I wanted to do before I could act. I hated feeling this way, and the drug had other maddening effects. Without warning sometimes I would realize that my lower lip was drooping, the saliva trickling from the corner of my mouth. I avoided taking the drugs whenever I could. Many times when given a capsule, I would put it in my mouth but outside my gum. Then, when the nurse turned her back, I would spit it out.

Not long after my arrival, a set of forty-year-old retarded

twins, Billy and Bobby, moved into our ward. I laughed at them at first—they were full-grown men but had the intelligence of six-year-olds. But before long I grew to care for them very much. Although their mental ability was limited, they were kind-hearted and gentle, and in certain activities, Billy and Bobby were brilliant. I taught them some table games, and once they learned the rules, their play was masterful. Both of them had an uncanny ability to recall dates of historical events. I would spend hours quizzing them and often had to verify their answers in an encyclopedia. They were seldom wrong. I adopted them as my special friends, ran errands for them, and took them for walks.

For two months I obeyed enough of the rules to keep almost everyone happy, and I didn't hit anybody. But finally I could take no more of Donny Horton. Donny was the overweight, babyish, whining sixteen-year-old I had met during my first meal at the institute. According to Donny, everyone took advantage of him and no one understood his unique problems. One afternoon, when Donny was belly-aching about one of the nurses, I confronted him.

"Donny, why don't you shut up for once and stand up for yourself," I said.

"Don't tell me what to do, Romeo," Donny said. He grabbed my shoulder and shoved me back. The second he touched me I hit him hard, just above the left eye. His face opened up, the blood washing down his cheek.

Four orderlies came running full speed. I expected the worst and attacked them with my fists and feet. I clenched one orderly around the neck and bit his ear. I kicked another between the legs. I knew they would win, but if I had to suffer a lot, I wanted them to suffer a little. The ruckus lasted less than a minute. I was wrestled to the floor and nearly disappeared under the bodies. When I was calmer, they wrapped me in a straitjacket. As they led me to the seclusion room, I saw the blood spattered on the shining, brown tile floor. Bright red spots and smears marred the white uniforms of the orderlies.

I was dumped on a bed in seclusion. The heavy dose of Thorazine they had needled into me when I was struggling took effect, and I collapsed, drifting into a two-day daze.

When I came out of it, my doctor entered the room.

"Are you going to behave yourself, Glenn?" Doctor Porter asked.

"Yes, Doctor," I answered meekly. I knew, though, my mental state was so shaky I no longer could guarantee my behavior. In spite of what I said, the doctor cancelled my privileges.

Before the incident with Donny I had made several friends among the other teen-agers. Now, disgusted with me because I had hit one of their buddies, they shunned me. I missed being with them, so I was forced to humble myself. I went and found Donny and apologized. Later we became friends. None of the other patients ever pushed me again.

Doctor Porter, the nurses, the medical students in training—all of them continued to probe and counsel me. After evaluating my history, the doctor said he believed my emotional problems had been caused by my frequent moves as a child and the abuse I had received in institutions.

My attitude always was that I was normal—it was the rest of the world, everyone else, who was crazy. But after several months of therapy I began to wonder. With staff members asking me day after day, "What can we do to help you?" I began to think, *Maybe I am crazy after all.*

It seemed the most helpful therapy came from my teenage friends. There weren't many patients our age, so we clanned together. Whenever life at the institute became too unbearable, we would "elope," a mental hospital word meaning "run away." Several times we were gone for a week.

On one elopement four of us went first to the home of one of those in our group, a guy named Johnny. We slipped into the house when his parents were gone and went directly to the bar. Johnny found a large suitcase, and we cleaned out the cabinet, packing the bag full of liquor bottles. We headed off for Times Square, and soon we were drunk. We stayed that way, wandering the streets until the booze was gone.

These unauthorized trips usually ended when we got tired or our panhandling near Times Square fizzled and we had no money for food. We would struggle back to the institute or be picked up by the police.

The other teen-agers and I sniffed glue whenever we could. Glue was easy to buy in the sixties, and on our elopements several of us would find a deserted roof of an apartment building and sniff ourselves high. One night I was so looped on glue I thought I could fly; and I did fly, leaping down from a thirty-step staircase. The flying was easy, but the landing on my knees and ankles made walking painful for several weeks.

At the institute my buddies and I stirred up as much fun as we could. Bored much of the time, we played table games or watched TV night after night. We listened to Top 40 music on the radio, and to amuse ourselves, we often wrote our own words to popular songs. One of our favorites was sung to the tune of "Heartbreak Hotel." Six of us would sing it boisterously off-key as we rumbled down the halls.

> Since my senses left me,
> I've found a new place to dwell;
> It's down on the end of Ft. Washington Street,
> Psychiatric hotel—
> Oh Baby, I'ma nuts over you, I'ma nuts over you. . . .

There were more verses, each one more obscene than the last. We seldom finished it; we began to giggle and the notes trailed off as we yelped with laughter.

One of my friends, Jack, had been a foster child like me. We often discussed our similar childhood experiences. Jack, who was twenty-one, was always deeply depressed. The black cloud he lived under never seemed to lift. Sometimes we talked about the future—I still hoped to learn a trade and live normally on the outside; but Jack saw only pain and failure ahead of him.

A team of three doctors worked with Jack, doggedly trying to break through his depression. Then without notice, and for no particular reason, Jack suddenly improved. In sessions with the doctors, he began to talk hopefully of the future and asked if he could start attending some college classes.

My friends and I knew he was putting on an act. Around us he was the same Jack, full of despair and angry with himself. My doctor was one of those treating Jack, and I told him that my friend was playing a game.

"Don't let Jack out of this place, Dr. Porter. He's going to hurt himself," I said. I often tried the doctor's patience, and this remark infuriated him.

"Why don't you mind your own business! We are the doctors. You are the patient," he snapped.

A bright, crisp November day, Jack was permitted to leave the institute to go register for his classes. He didn't come back.

Three days later the staff called a special ward meeting. Dr. Porter and two other doctors walked in and sat down, facing us. One of them, in a low, steady voice, announced that Jack's body had been found in the Hudson River. He had jumped from the George Washington Bridge.

I grieved for Jack, and the news frightened me, weakening my stomach. I trembled in fear because I, too, slipped so often into the black pit of depression. *Will I kill myself, too?* I thought.

Shaking, I stood and walked to the three doctors. "You people are nothin' but a bunch of murderers!" I said. "You're not going to kill me like you killed Jack." I spit in Dr. Porter's face and walked out.

Months passed. Each level of my treatment became just another step toward failure. Dr. Porter tried everything— more privileges, less privileges; more drugs, less drugs; friendly chats, confrontations. The doctor wanted to give me shock treatments, but my stepfather Tom wouldn't let

Mother give written permission. I would control myself for a while; but then the frustration or depression would build and I would blow up, run away, or bother a nurse. Sometimes I ran to visit my former foster mother Mrs. Brown. I wanted to see the Winstons, but I had lost contact with them. But it was my bothering of nurses, especially the student nurses, that finally ended my stay at the institute.

I had a polished series of tricks I used to get attention from each new batch of student nurses rotating into psychiatric training. One afternoon a girl named Sherrie was nervously spending her first shift in the "psych ward." I was slumped in a chair in a long hall, apparently dozing. I sneaked a look and saw Sherrie approaching, her general anxiety showing in the rigid way she walked.

When she was fifteen feet away, I began to breathe heavily, raising the volume, depth, and speed of each breath as she neared. When she pulled even with me, now quickening her steps and looking worriedly from the corner of her eye, I poured on the passion, ending each exhale with a longing moan. After Sherrie passed, I wailed uncontrollably, leaped from my chair, and bolted after her. "I want you, I want you!" I howled.

Poor Sherrie screamed for help and ran down the hall, her worst fears about crazy sex maniacs fulfilled. I stopped and doubled over with laughter.

I suppose the student nurses, when they caught on to my game, were mildly amused by this behavior. But an older lady, a permanent nurse on the ward, did not find me funny at all. Her name was Janice Peoples. She was a tall, slender, thin-lipped woman who lived her life by the books. She thrived in the well-ordered hospital environment and had a rule for me to break every minute of the day. I despised her. And although she would have never admitted it, I know she felt the same way about me.

"That's inappropriate behavior, *Mister Hester,*" Nurse Peoples would say after I had put my arm around a student nurse. She would always whine the words out in a high-pitched voice, saying the "Mister Hester" with a sniff. Having judged, convicted, and executed me, she would glare at me, hands on hips, her lips drawn tight in a thin red line. She was in her forties, and after years at the hospital she had been so worn down that she was taking everybody—especially herself—too seriously. She always seemed to be hovering near me, ready to pounce.

Dances were held at the hospital every month. I was a good dancer and looked forward to these evenings, spending an hour in preparation, scenting my body, combing my hair, and dressing so I would be my alluring best. Some student nurses always came. I guess they were required once during their psychiatric training to observe the "psychos" at play. As the records started to spin, I would cajole a young nurse out on the floor. Whether the music was fast or slow, I had the moves and was foolhardy enough to get dangerously close to my partner. Sometimes I would draw a nurse into a clinch and blow in her ear without missing a step. Nurse Peoples, standing with arms folded at the edge of the floor, didn't miss a step either, and in an instant she would be tapping me on the shoulder: "That's inappropriate behavior, *Mister Hester!*"

"Hey, Peoples, stick it in your ear!"

"*That's* very inappropriate language, *Mister Hester;* I'm going to report you to the doctor."

I would shrug my shoulders and walk off.

In September, nearly a year after I entered the institute, I met a student nurse I really liked, and in a good-natured, "I-want-to-help-the-kid" way, she liked me.

One afternoon I was cutting wood with an electric saw in the occupational therapy shop. The safety guard on the saw jammed, and when I grasped it, the whirling blade caught my fingers, gashing them deeply. I was rushed to the emergency room in the medical section of the hospital. As the doctor was sewing in fifteen stitches, a young nurse stood beside me, comforting me in a pleasant way. She had no idea I was a mental patient.

"You're a student nurse, aren't you?" I said.

"Yes," she answered.

"What's your next class?" I had a hunch what her answer would be.

"Psychiatry."

After the doctor finished, I paused on the way out and said in an expectant voice to the nurse: "I'll see you next month . . . I'm over on the psych ward!"

She did come some weeks later, and our rapport developed nicely. Her name was LaVonne Green. She was a small, fine-boned girl who was full of fun.

One afternoon in mid-December, two weeks after LaVonne came on the ward, I was chasing her playfully around a ping pong table. For once this behavior on my part was essentially harmless. We were just having a good time. I reached for her wrist, and as I closed my fingers, she turned the wrong way and we heard a snap. She screamed. Her arm was broken, and in seconds the orderlies poured in on me, grabbing my shoulders and arms. I tried a few words of explanation, but it seemed no one was listening. So I lashed out with my fists, thudding repeatedly into their chests and arms.

The orderlies dragged me to the padded seclusion room. Two hours later my doctor showed up.

"Glenn, this is a serious matter. We're going to have to evaluate your situation here," he said. I sensed the end was near.

Before he left, Dr. Porter released me from seclusion. As I passed by the nurses' station, Nurse Peoples stood behind the counter, hands on hips, her face glowing with satisfaction.

"I see you finally got yourself in trouble," she said to me in her high voice, condemnation oozing from each word.

"Drop dead, Peoples," I answered.

"That's inappropriate language, *Mister Hester*. Because of that I'm going to cancel your Christmas leave to go home," she said triumphantly, a bit of her rage peeking out.

The anger inside of me burst. I walked to her and smashed my fist against the left side of her face. She fell backwards to the floor. I jumped toward her, wanting to finish her off. Again the orderlies came, and again I fought back. This time I was bound with handcuffs and sent up a floor to the maximum security ward.

I never returned to my old ward. The kidding of student nurses, the singing of songs with my buddies, the running away to Times Square was over.

In maximum security a leather strap bound my hands at all times. I had to have someone light my cigarettes, and an orderly sat near me twenty-four hours a day.

After three weeks, the administration convinced Mother to sign more papers, and I was sent to another mental hospital—a maximum security facility with all doors locked and windows barred. Before I left the institute, one of my black friends, John Johnson, was brought up to my new ward.

"What are you doin' here, Johnson?" I asked.

He smiled. "After ya left, old Nurse Peoples ran her mouth about what an 'in'propriate' dude ya were and what had happened to ya would happen to anybody who did 'in-'propriate' things. I got tired of her mouth and knocked her out m'self. I got the other side of her face, kind of even'd it up."

We laughed uproariously.

Two weeks later we didn't laugh at all as we both rode a bus to Rockland State Hospital, a dismal place filled with sad, unpredictable, sick people.

8. Runaway

Orangeburg, New York, the 1960s

Rockland State Hospital made the Psychiatric Institute by comparison seem a luxurious resort hotel. At Rockland, no one played games or tried to understand me. It was a closely guarded, brick-walled prison where my main therapy was hard work.

Johnson and I were processed in by a pale, weak-looking man who was barricaded behind a massive gray metal desk. We sat on two steel folding chairs facing him while he sullenly spat out the Rockland regulations. Two tall orderlies stared at us, one standing on either side of the frail interviewer.

I was not impressed with the man or his speech and gazed above his face at a brown water mark on the ceiling. He ignored my inattention for about a minute before he jumped to his feet, walked quickly around his desk, and grabbed my hair, jerking my head down.

"You look at me, you scummy punk!" he yelled. "You pull any of the crap you pulled at the Psychiatric Institute, and we're going to lock you up for a thousand years—you hear me?"

I didn't say anything, but I wanted to laugh. I wasn't afraid of him or his bodyguards.

Johnson and I were assigned to a juvenile ward where, except for us, the oldest boy was twelve. Some of the inmates were as young as six. Being less dependent than the others, Johnson and I were put to work from 6:00 A.M. to 11:00 P.M. each day, sweeping floors, washing down latrines, and scraping feces from soiled sheets.

After being at Rockland a week, I was allowed one afternoon to run to the hospital canteen for a soda. When I walked in, I saw two teen-age boys and a girl who looked familiar. I was shocked when I realized all of them had been with me at Pinewood Farms. They recognized me, too, and we greeted each other excitedly, exchanging hugs. For a few minutes we reminisced bitterly about our problems at Pinewood.

I was sad having met these former acquaintances at a place like Rockland, but comforted too. I knew now I wasn't the only one who had been twisted emotionally during my childhood years in an institution.

Johnson and I worked without relief in the children's ward, and finally our spirits broke, more from fatigue than anything else. After six weeks, both of us were moved to an adult ward. Memories of the horrors of that human garbage dump still frighten and nauseate me.

The ward was a large, high-ceilinged room. Neon lights, their long tubes bare and always humming, cast a blue-green light. About one hundred men were cramped together there. Long rows of steel-framed beds were separated by narrow aisles, and crumbling pieces of wood furniture were scattered along the walls. Open radiators, layered with many coats of green paint, stood every few feet beneath windows protected by steel mesh and bars. All of the walls at Rockland were painted green. A dark brown tile covered the floors, which were washed and buffed daily.

The morning Johnson and I arrived on the ward, a middle-aged-looking man, his brown hair thinned out and gray at the edges, padded up to within about six feet of me and stopped.

"Hey, you sweet looking thing; how would you like a free carton of cigarettes?" he asked me in a sugary, inviting voice.

I knew he was homosexual. I decided to stop his advances fast. I swore at him, took three steps, and kicked him as hard as I could between the legs. As he doubled over with a groan, three guards grabbed me, knocking me to the floor.

A leather strap was brought, and my hands were bound in front of me.

With my hands tied, I could not defend myself very well, which scared me. I had to shuffle sideways, constantly turning my head from side to side to see who was coming and from which direction. Otherwise I might be knocked down and raped.

I was only fifteen years old but was seeing twisted, perverted behavior most adults would not believe possible. We received no treatment, except for the twice daily dose of drugs. I hardly ever swallowed my pills. After the nurse passed, I would spit out the capsules and later give them to someone else. Some of the men were desperate for stronger doses of medicine. I helped them as much as I could.

Some of the older patients had been in the hospital for nearly a lifetime. They aimlessly wandered around, without warning screaming or breaking into a crying spell. I became desperate and plotted escape plans for hours on end, but there seemed to be no way out. I was trapped.

The short-haired orderlies, wearing their starched white uniforms and shiny black shoes, hurried around in groups of two or three, ready in a moment to unleash their violence. When the guards were bored, they would trump up a reason to stage a cockfight between two patients. Some guards were homosexuals who amused themselves by cornering unwary patients.

I constantly feared rape. You had to be careful, never allowing yourself to be caught alone and vulnerable. The shower rooms were the most dangerous—you already had your clothes off. Johnson and I always showered at the same time. The guards and other patients knew we would fight to protect ourselves.

After three weeks the leather straps on my wrists were removed. I had now been at Rockland nearly two months. I had to get out. My anxiety about staying leaped when Johnson's parents came and took him home. Before leaving he told me, "Glenn, if you're goin' to get out of this place, don't hit nobody no more."

I was alone, and although I despised the thought, I realized only Mother could sign my release. I arranged for her to visit me, and when she came, I covered my pride. I grasped her hand and knelt before her.

"Mother, I'm sorry I hit you. I'll never do it again, and I'll be good." I didn't mean a word I said, but she believed me. A few days later she returned. I was released, the only stipulation being that I return monthly for out-patient counseling.

Mother and Tom were now living north of New York City in the small town of Sparkill. Since it was April and near the end of the school year, I was unable to enroll in high school. Tom found me a job digging graves at a cemetery near an orphanage where he worked as a maintenance supervisor. Swinging a pick and digging with a shovel was hard work, but I enjoyed being free, spending time out of doors and using my physical strength. And the pay was good—$110 a week.

Mother and I coexisted without trouble until my first payday. I was paid in cash on Friday night after work. When I walked out of the cemetery office with my wages still in the envelope, Mother was waiting for me. In the car she asked to see the money. I handed it to her, and she counted the bills, finally giving me back a five-dollar bill. "That's for your expenses. I'm keeping the rest for your rent," she said. I began to burn.

Each Friday night Mother appeared, and the same events occurred; each time my anger grew.

One Friday night in June, Mother was delayed, and I brought the $110 home myself. Quickly I showered, dressed, and caught a bus into the city. After walking Times Square for an hour or two, I bought some pot and smoked it to relax. Several hours later I ended up at the bus station. I sat down on a bench and pulled what remained of my cash from my pocket, about ninety dollars. As I looked at the bills—the money Mother would grab as soon as I returned home—I decided it was time to leave town.

I wanted to budget my money, so I walked to a ticket window and asked the agent: "How far south can I go on fifteen dollars?"

The man flipped through his schedule book some moments before replying, "For seventeen dollars you can get a ticket to Raleigh, North Carolina." He looked at me blankly, unconcerned that I was a young kid who was obviously about to split town.

"One ticket to Raleigh, North Carolina," I said, sliding the bills across the counter.

At midnight my bus headed south, the city lights fading as we crossed the bridge and rumbled into New Jersey. I felt good, glad to be on my own again. It bothered me not at all that Mother and Tom would once again have to put the police on my tail.

The next morning I arrived in Raleigh. By 9:00 A.M. it was already hot; the heat blasted my face as I stepped down from the bus. The rest of the day I spent wandering through the city. I liked the old, large homes with their heavily wooded yards, the flowering trees and bushes. In the afternoon I bought a razor and some soap. By sundown I was exhausted and collapsed on the bed of a flophouse room I rented near the center of town.

For about a week I lazed about, my money dribbling away until the last dollar was gone. After nearly two days without food and some nights of sleeping in alleys, I needed a job. I walked down a residential street, stopping in front of a home large enough to be a mansion. The grass needed cutting, and the yard was littered with tree limbs broken during a recent rainstorm. I walked to the front door and knocked. Footsteps sounded on the other side, the lock clicked open, and when the door swung in I looked into the face of a trim, middle-aged woman.

"Hello," she said, her voice gently sweetening and stretching the syllables as Southern matrons often do. The skin on her face was a delicate pink and looked soft. Her gaze was steady, her green eyes appraising me serenely.

"Ma'am, I'd be glad to clear your whole lawn and cut

your grass if I could have a sandwich." I hurried the words out, my raspy New York accent jarring the tranquil scene.

The woman paused; I had spoken so rapidly she needed a moment to figure out what I had said.

"Honey," she said, "are you an orphan?"

"Yeah, how'd you know?"

"I'm not sure, dear, you just look like an orphan to me. You come in now and sit down at the table in the kitchen," she said, swinging wide the door. "I'll make you a sandwich and pay you when you're done with the yard."

We visited politely as she prepared several items of food and spread them before me. I tried to watch my manners, but my hands were shaking from hunger and I wolfed down the meal. The woman sat erectly across from me, smiling frequently, her eyes warm and unwary.

It took me most of the afternoon to cut and clean the yard. When I finished, the woman fed me supper. After the meal she handed me a ten-dollar bill.

"Thank you, Ma'am," I said appreciatively. I knew ten bucks would keep me afloat for at least two days.

"Glenn, are you looking for a job?" she said softly.

"Yes, Ma'am, but I don't know where to look in this town."

"Why don't you go over to the Royal Carriage Hotel. I've heard they need someone to help in the kitchen," she said.

She wished me luck and watched from the long porch as I walked off. I felt confident again; my stomach was full and ten dollars padded my pocket.

At the hotel, a first-class, shining facility, I learned I wasn't needed in the kitchen, but the maintenance man, Ralph, needed help and took me on. He introduced me to a young man who stayed in a nearby boarding house, and he and I agreed to split the rent on his room. In a matter of hours I had found a job and a place to live.

My stay in Raleigh was tranquil, a lull from the storms of my life. At the hotel I swept halls, washed windows, picked up trash, cut grass, and helped Ralph with other maintenance jobs. After work and in the evenings, I would drift into Johnny's Tavern for a beer or two. I told everyone at the bar I was eighteen—and I probably looked it. The anxious, violent days in my past had hardened my face. My hair was styled like an adult's, and I acted tough and worldly. I knew how to intimidate others with a look or well-timed word. When people looked at me, a little fear showed in their eyes. But inside I was more scared than anybody, desperately afraid that someone would get to know me and see my weaknesses.

Life was good, though, and I even found a girl friend, a waitress named Denise. Some nights I would stay with her, not going home to my ten-dollar-a-week room. My meals were furnished at the hotel, and I was paid sixty dollars a week. I never considered returning to New York.

Nearly three months passed. Back home the police were dragging the rivers; many people thought I had finally gotten rid of myself. Mother and Tom sent my old buddies into the city to search for me in Greenwich Village and around Times Square. I had vanished without a clue.

One afternoon in September I was walking home from work, whistling along, enjoying the warm, fall weather. When I reached the block where I lived, I saw a police car parked in front of my boarding house. My heart began to pound, and I ducked into a corner drugstore. I bought a soda and sipped it, looking through the window, watching my house until the police left.

I hurried home. My landlady met me at the door.

"You better get out of here," she said. "The police were here asking about a 'runaway boy.' They want me to call when I see you. I won't, but you better get going."

I ran upstairs and grabbed my things. Ten minutes later I left for the hotel. There I found my boss; he paid me what the hotel owed me out of his own pocket and wished me luck.

I hiked to the bus station and learned the next bus south was leaving in twenty-two minutes. I bought a ticket. A half hour later I was out of town, leaving, I hoped, no tracks anyone could follow. I never found out who tipped off the cops about my being in Raleigh.

On the Florida-bound bus, two girls sitting across the aisle from me turned out to be runaways, too. We talked for a while. By the time the bus reached Miami, we were friends and checked into a motel room together.

In a few days my money ran out, and soon after, so did the girls. I found ways to survive—washing dishes in a restaurant for a meal, cleaning lawns for a couple of bucks. At night I slept under a stack of benches on the beach. When I needed a shave I slipped into the restroom of a service station. New York seemed far enough away to be in another world. I thought no one could catch me.

One hot, sticky night I didn't bother to find a bench to sleep under and just stretched out on the open sand. At 2:00 A.M. a light in my face awakened me. Standing above me with flashlights and billy clubs were two policemen. I had no identification on me—I had lost my billfold—and I refused to say who I was. They searched me and found my six-inch, folding-blade knife. Just for that the policemen hauled me to the Dade County juvenile center.

I still wouldn't talk, so I was locked into a windowless, dark closet. Inside the temperature must have been above one hundred degrees. The air was dead and it stunk. I lasted twelve hours before my thirst and an awesome need to relieve myself forced me to give in. "I'm ready to talk now," I shouted through the door.

I told them my name and admitted I was a runaway from New York City. A turnkey made me strip off my clothes, and I was doused with a liquid disinfectant and dusted heavily with flea powder. I was locked stark naked in a private cell for five days. The jailers wanted to be certain I wouldn't spread any infectious disease I might be carrying.

Mother and Tom were called. My vacation was over. Three weeks passed before the money for my ticket home arrived. I was escorted to the airport and put on a plane. It was now November; I had been gone for five months.

After landing at Kennedy Airport, I was met by Mother and Tom. Mother was not happy to see me.

"Did you have a good time?" she asked sarcastically.

"It was just by chance I got caught," I muttered.

Mother decided to discipline me a little and grabbed my ear, giving it a twist. I squirmed and clenched my fists.

"You better take your hands off him," Tom said, a hint of both warning and fear in his voice.

My folks took me to the police station to prove I was alive. An officer there warned me that the next time I ran the police would send me to jail. His words didn't intimidate me. The law and its keepers no longer impressed me.

I went back to school, enrolling in a vocational high school to study plumbing. In the plumbing courses I made straight A's. The other classes I flunked.

The family still lived in Sparkill, a village that offered me little amusement. Mother didn't bother me for a while, but after a few weeks she had me cleaning the house, washing clothes, and doing anything she could think of to "straighten out the bad boy." I hated being pushed around by her.

Terribly bored and anxious to get out of the house, I attended a small Episcopal church pastored by a young priest, "Reverend Sam" I called him. I didn't want to like him—I expected such a "holy man" to be weak—but his youthful, friendly manner won me over. Reverend Sam liked dressing in jeans and tee shirts and being with us kids.

I began to share things about myself with the pastor, cracking slightly the cover on my buried feelings. One day he asked me, "Glenn, have you ever had a real friend?"

"Nope," I answered without hesitation.

"I'll be your friend if you want me to."

After that I trusted Reverend Sam a little. I didn't let him get too close, but I didn't shut him out either. I spent many hours helping him at the church, painting and making repairs.

About Thanksgiving Mother started irritating me again.

"Tom," I said to my stepfather one evening, "I'm sixteen years old, and I don't want her putting her hands on me, pushing me around."

Tom took Mother aside. I heard him say firmly, "I'll discipline the boy." She didn't like this, and in a few minutes they were arguing. I could not bear this and stomped out of the house. Seeing me leave, Mother thought I was running away again. She called the police.

I was a mile up the road, walking to a friend's house, when a squad car pulled beside me. "Hold it! Get in the car," the cop on the passenger side growled as he jumped out. He pushed me against the car door. "You're running away again, aren't you?"

I was befuddled. I didn't know Mother had called the police. They took me home and nothing happened, but I began to plan again how I would get away.

I was still attending the out-patient clinic at Rockland State Hospital once a month. The counselor I saw there always asked if I had any problems. I always answered no. I knew if I said yes, he might commit me to the hospital again. I waited as patiently as I could, deciding it was better to endure Mother than to rejoin the loonies at Rockland.

At school one morning in December, another student and I traded insults in the woodworking shop. He gave me a shove. I reacted in the violent way I knew best, smashing the side of his head with a two-by-four I was holding. The principal ejected me from school and sent me home.

It was an icy cold day, and since Mother and Tom didn't trust me alone in their house, I had no door key. I was forced to stand outside shivering most of the day. First I tried to find shelter at the homes of friends, but everyone I knew was gone, even Reverend Sam. Then I wandered around the town, slipping into a store to warm myself for as long as I could before the store owner grew suspicious. I would be forced to go outside again.

When Mother and Tom finally came home after dark, I was tired, and shaking and numb from the cold. Mother started right in with a lecture, not wanting to hear a word from me.

"I got a phone call from school. They said you hit a kid," she said. Mother slapped me across the mouth.

My restraint vanished. I hit her back—hard—in the mouth. One punch wasn't enough so I gave her more. I wanted to hurt her, to get back at her for some of the wounds of my childhood. I swung several times; she screamed. Tom grabbed my shoulder, then I started beating on him too. When my fury was spent, Mother was terrified, unwilling to have me stay another day in her house. She knew I might kill her, and she was right. The police were called again.

The officers came several minutes later. I packed a small bag and rode alone, handcuffed, in the back seat of the cruiser to Rockland State Hospital. When I saw the dark, brick wall and the concrete buildings, I sickened with dread. In the admissions office I asked if I could make a phone call. The clerk pointed me to a desk phone. I called Reverend Sam.

"Sam, you gotta get me out of here. Please come see me," I pleaded.

"Glenn, I'll be there tomorrow."

I was totally beside myself now. The beaches of Miami and the warm, fragrant evenings of freedom in Raleigh seemed but cruel dreams. I was sixteen years old, and I knew that I had no chance of leaving Rockland until I was at least eighteen.

Sam came the next day. We talked, and he thought of an idea. Sam went back to Sparkill and visited with Mother. He pleaded, urging her to find another home for me, some new environment, any place far away from Rockland and from her. Sam knew my life might depend on it.

Mother thought for a while and then remembered some people who once had cared for me. She called Uncle Hank and Aunt Sarah, now living in Waynesboro, Virginia.

"Would it be all right if Glenn came to live with you for a time? He's having some trouble in school here," Mother said, neglecting to mention I was living in a mental hospital.

"Why . . . Sure, send him down," Hank answered.

In January Mother signed me out of Rockland. A few days later Hank and Sarah arrived from Virginia. I packed a suitcase and said my good-byes. It had taken fifteen years, but Sarah and Hank finally had me back again.

9. Shine My Shoes, Boy

Waynesboro, Virginia, the 1960s

Waynesboro nestles in the foothills of the Blue Ridge Mountains in Virginia. When I arrived the small city had a population of about fifteen thousand. On the surface Waynesboro looked quiet, clean, and harmless. Reverend Sam had certainly arranged a new environment for me, a drastic change from the frantic pace of New York City.

As we entered the city limits, Uncle Hank and Aunt Sarah pointed out landmarks. Hank said that a Civil War battle had been fought at Waynesboro, a victory for the North won by a general named George Custer. I smiled, thoroughly happy to be away from Mother and Rockland State Hospital.

Hank was a machinist, a likable, no-surprises solid citizen. He and Sarah lived in a medium-sized house in a middle-class neighborhood. When we reached their home, Sarah helped me organize my few clothes and personal articles in a small room. I settled in.

My aunt and uncle wanted me to attend school. My first Monday in Virginia I walked to Waynesboro High School and introduced myself to the school's guidance counselor, Mrs. Martha Schneider, a pert, talkative, slightly graying lady. We chatted a few minutes; she soon told me I could not enroll without paying tuition if I did not have a letter from Mother showing that Hank and Sarah were my guardians.

That evening I called Mother, asking her to send the letter. She said she would right away, but I knew from past experience that she might procrastinate. I waited about

ten days and then decided to get a job. I found one at a
fast-service hamburger shop.

I fried hamburgers at the restaurant for a few weeks
without incident. The assistant manager of the place,
Charles Treney, worked there as a moonlighter. He was a
big man, six feet two, two hundred pounds. Charlie enjoyed
being a boss and yelling out orders, strutting through the
kitchen, acting like he knew what a manager should do. He
was pompous, in a simple, unintentional way, and one slow
night the other teen-age workers and I sprung a practical
joke on him.

There were two telephones on the premises, a pay phone
outdoors for customers and a desk phone back in the office.
One of the workers slipped outside and dialed the number
of the phone in the office. Charlie answered. The boy lowered his voice, pretending to be a foreman calling from a
local factory. He placed an order for two hundred hamburgers "to go" to be picked up in twenty-five minutes.

Charlie slammed the phone down, scribbled the order on
the back of an envelope, and ran gleefully to the kitchen.

"Hey, get busy, we need to fry two hundred burgers by
8:30," he cried, unable to restrain his excitement and pride
over such an impressive order.

The restaurant was almost empty, and the kitchen help-
ers were standing by, leaning on counters or squatting on
the floor. I was at the grill, and when Charlie bounced in, I
looked at him curiously and sighed, making no move at all.
Everyone else also stayed motionless with bored looks on
their faces. Several of us wanted to laugh and were fighting to keep control.

Charlie became quite annoyed. "Get the lead out!" he
yelled. "The guy will be here in twenty minutes."

"We don't feel like doing it. Why can't the guy go some
place else?" a boy said, squelching a laugh in his throat at
the last second.

Charlie swore viciously and ran across the kitchen; he
began slapping meat patties on the grill. Perspiration
gleamed on his forehead. I couldn't bridle myself a moment

longer. I began to laugh. "Hey, man," I yelled at him, "it's only a joke. There's nobody comin'."

We all doubled over in laughter—except Charlie. I couldn't stop laughing; I knew I should, but I just couldn't. Every time I looked at Charlie standing there with his mouth open, the smoke billowing from the frying hamburgers, I broke down. The others stopped, but I went on, barking with laughter, gasping for air, banging my spatula on the grill. Charlie didn't like my laughing so long. The red in his face deepened, and then he grabbed my collar, twisting it tight on my neck.

"At nine o'clock when you get off, I'm meeting you outside, Hester," he said.

I stopped laughing. "Oh, yeah?" I said, pulling away. I wasn't mad, though, and quickly forgot what he had said. I was used to having people threaten me, and I expected Charlie to cool down and forget.

At nine I punched out on the time clock and washed up. When I opened the employee door to leave, Charlie was standing on the other side. He greeted me with his right fist—in my mouth. He swarmed on me, his huge frame swallowing up my 145-pound, five feet nine body. I had a pocket knife and slipped it out between blows. When Charlie lunged again I started cutting him. He began to bleed but didn't stop flailing away. I grew more angry and was preparing to stick him, to kill him, when the restaurant's manager, who just had come on duty, came running. He grabbed my knife hand and slammed it repeatedly against the brick wall until I let go.

The manager released me; I knew the fight was over, so I started for home, leaving the knife behind.

Back at Hank and Sarah's, I visited for a few minutes with them and then went to bed. Later, at 1:00 A.M., a policeman knocked at the door. Uncle Hank answered.

"Is Glenn Hester here?" the officer asked.

"Yes. Why, what's the problem?"

"He stabbed a man. We need to talk to him," the policeman said.

I was awakened and brought sleepy-eyed to the door. Uncle Hank looked on in disbelief as I admitted knifing Charlie.

"You mean you came home as quiet as can be and didn't even tell us you stabbed somebody?" Hank asked, shaking his head in wonder.

"I had a problem and I settled it. I don't bring my work home," I answered, shrugging my bare shoulders.

The police told me to be in court the next morning. We went back to bed. I imagine my uncle and aunt talked for a good while and didn't sleep much. They were beginning to realize that Mother had dumped an emotional timebomb into their laps.

The next morning in court, to my surprise Charlie admitted hitting me first. He was bandaged and sore from the cuts, which had required twenty-four stitches to close. The judge first bawled out Charlie for swinging first, and then he raked me for using a knife. He decided to free both of us until a detailed investigation could be completed.

The fight ended my job frying hamburgers, so I tried once more to enroll in school. I visited with Mrs. Schneider. I liked talking to her, and we were becoming friends; but she still could not permit me to start school tuition-free. It was already April—I had lived in Waynesboro three months—but Mother's letter of authorization had not come.

Later on the same day Mrs. Schneider and I had talked again, a man who owned a local hardware store stopped by the house to see me. This fellow had heard about me, and since he enjoyed helping "kids in trouble," he offered me a job. I took it.

At the store I helped assemble fishing gear, ran the key-making machine, and swept floors. My favorite activity was handling sporting goods, especially guns. I loved guns. While out hunting with a cousin I had recently found I was a naturally accurate marksman. Guns represented a power my fists could not generate. The rifles and pistols at the store were locked in cases, but I was able to steal a high-powered BB gun and hid it in the stock room.

One day I took the BB gun and climbed to the deserted top floor of the building. I poured BBs into the barrel and peered out a window at the street. The hardware store was near downtown, and street traffic was heavy. It was past noon, a sunny, pleasant spring afternoon. The sidewalks were crowded with shoppers. Gazing at the street, I thought of one of my heroes—Lee Harvey Oswald—and how he had sat in a building like this and showed the world what just one dedicated, desperate person could do to get even with society.

Down below I saw a plump, middle-aged woman ambling away from me on the sidewalk, a large grocery sack cradled in her right arm. I cocked the gun, aimed at the woman's elbow, and fired. The BB stung her elbow, she yelped, and the grocery bag dropped to the pavement, eggs breaking, fruit rolling into the gutter. The woman stood rubbing her arm while other passersby gathered her groceries.

Ducking down beneath the window I laughed until tears streamed down my cheeks. I calmed down and waited until my first victim was gone—along with the witnesses.

A convertible, its top down, drew up to the traffic light and stopped. The driver was a young man, obviously enjoying the mild weather. As he waited for the light to change, I cocked again and drew a bead on the back of his head. Gently I squeezed the trigger. The shot richocheted off the man's skull. He jumped, whipped his hand to the sore spot, and shook his head back and forth as if stunned. He turned and looked behind him. I could tell he was angry. I didn't laugh very long this time and quickly rehid the gun and went back to the main floor to work. The young man in the convertible called the police, and two officers came and talked to him.

Two days later, feeling bold again, I loaded the gun and returned to my post. Another convertible with top down came along. I took aim again, my body trembling as I began to snicker with anticipation. I sighted the driver's head, pulled the trigger—and missed. The BB struck the windshield and it cracked. The driver slammed his brakes and leaped from the car. Seeing the hole in the window he turned completely around, trying to determine from where the shot had come. His eyes settled on the top floor of the hardware store. The police were summoned again. They came, and this time they soon found me and solved the crime. I was jailed, much to the embarrassment of Hank and Sarah.

Now I was in deep trouble. Since I had been charged only weeks before with a felony in the knifing incident, this time the judge decided I needed a professional evaluation of my mental stability.

Four days later I was taken by car to Southwestern State Hospital, a mental institution for the criminally insane at Marion, Virginia. Only four months had passed since my last stay at Rockland.

Although I was sent to Southwestern supposedly just for testing and counseling, the way I was treated it would have been no worse being sentenced there permanently. The hospital was a maximum security prison, filled with dangerous men, many of them serving life sentences for murder.

When I arrived I was orientated by a loud-voiced, pale-cheeked man with an extremely short crewcut. His teeth were browned by coffee and cigarette stains. He paced rapidly about the room, his body stiff except for his shoulders which jerked back and forth crudely. His name was Fred Stamp.

Mr. Stamp listed the rules at Southwestern, which were about the same as those at Rockland: "Do as you're told." He stressed in particular, "If anyone is planning to break out of this place, and you know about it and don't tell the guards, when the escapee is caught, you'll suffer equal punishment."

After my lecture, two guards led me to a dressing room

where I was forced to take off every piece of clothing. The men searched every inch of my body for contraband, digging through my hair, making me spread my "cheeks," and even carefully probing between each of my toes. They found nothing. I was given a denim prison uniform.

The environment at Southwestern was tense and highly regimented. Security measures were tight. My first week was spent in a ward for newcomers where we were expected to learn proper manners. I learned that before I could stand up, sit down, or make any kind of move, I had to raise a hand and seek specific permission from an attendant.

During my first full day in the ward, a group of about fifty of us were sitting quietly in a large room, watched by attendants who looked eager to pounce at the sign of an infraction. I raised my hand.

"Hester?" a 220-pound, paunchy attendant barked.

"Yes, sir!" I snapped, rising to my feet immediately. This act was required before a patient could address a request to an attendant.

"Request to go to bathroom, sir."

"Go."

In the bathroom, while I was washing my hands, another patient stealthily approached me and said in a whisper, "Your name Hester?"

I nodded.

"You cut up a guy who works in a mental hospital, didn't you?"

"How'd you know?" I asked, puzzled by his knowledge of me.

"Just be careful. They're going to set you up."

The man left, saying no more. Later, I realized the staffers at Southwestern had read my records. They knew I had knifed Charlie who, when he wasn't managing the hamburger shop, worked as an orderly at a mental institution. I was marked. I had hurt one of their own kind.

The men who worked on staff in the wards at Southwestern were for the most part tall, heavy men who had been molded by the hospital environment into rigid, rules-bound, unfeeling robots. Pay at the hospital was poor, the highest scale being eighty-three dollars a week. The low wages and depressing conditions attracted only the poorly educated and those who could not hold better jobs elsewhere. Inside the walls of Southwestern State, many of these dull-witted men became drunk on their own power and paraded around like sultans. Typically, it wasn't long before my smart mouth and rebellious ways got me in trouble.

The day after the furtive conversation in the restroom, one of the orderlies, red-faced, 250-pound John Davis, decided to give me a hard time. I was reading a magazine, which I quickly put down when he bellowed out my name.

"Yes, sir," I said, standing up.

"Come heah, boy," Big John ordered in his hillbilly drawl. I walked to where he stood and froze at attention two paces in front of him. He stared beyond me, not acknowledging me. I stood there, erect as a Marine, for five minutes. I already had learned not to move or to speak without permission.

"Hester! See that shoebox theah?" John said finally.

"Yes, sir."

"Bringt ovah heah. You shine mah shoes, boy."

"What?" I answered indignantly. The way I said it, in a defiant tone of voice, was a mistake. Instantly John and three other guards cornered me and started pushing.

"You goin' to git an education, boy!" one of them whined. For once I didn't use my fists when shoved. I dropped to my knees and shined Big John's already gleaming black shoes. When I finished, Big John flipped a dime on the floor.

"That's for you. I don't want nobody tellin' me I made you do somethin' you didn't wanna do. You asked to shine mah shoes, didn't you, *boy?*"

"Yes, sir," I snapped, thinking how I would like to cut his tongue out.

"You needed that dime, didn't you, *Mister* Hester?" John said, laughing as he walked away.

They always gave you a dime. It was a little game for them, a diversion. None of the prisoners could later accuse the guards of forcing someone to do personal favors free of charge.

Weeks passed, but still I received no psychiatric evaluation. In the meantime I shined shoes and tried to obey the rules. After a month I was transferred to a more lenient ward. Even there, though, we were watched constantly by attendants and television cameras.

Three days after coming to the new ward, I was playing cards in the morning with three other prisoners. One of the players in low tones asked me if I wanted to "get out of this joint." I knew the rules against keeping quiet about escape plans, and I had no idea if this guy meant it or was just a stoolie setting me up.

"Forget it," I said, finally. The card game continued without other such comments.

Two days later the same inmate asked again if I wanted out. This time I showed some interest, and he explained the plan. Four of us would make the break, which was planned for Father's Day night a couple of weeks away. Hopefully, fewer guards would be on duty since most of them had families and would request the day off. I had been chosen because of my background—"good at starting fights." I was to pick a fight with someone in a bathroom. This ruckus would attract three of the four guards expected to be on duty. The three other prisoners breaking out would overpower the remaining guard and snatch his keys. The doors would be opened, and we would get other prisoners to boost us over the fence that bordered the grounds.

Escape sounded good to me. Weeks had gone by, and no one seemed to remember I was there or know when I might leave. I worried that I might never get out. I was a seventeen-year-old kid and wanted to be free. My partners in the break were older. Two of them were murderers—one had slit his mother's throat. Partly out of dread, I agreed to help them. I didn't want to risk saying no to any of them.

Father's Day came, and soon after breakfast, Mr. Stamp

strutted into the ward and called out the names of eight persons he wanted to see immediately. I was in the group, and so were my three buddies. I suspected there would be no breakout this Father's Day. We lined up in front of the smug-looking man.

"I understand you all are planning on taking a vacation," Stamp said, marching up and down before us, his voice quivering with excitement. "Certainly you men don't want to leave us!"

I watched him, expressionless. My heart was sinking; I knew the coming hours would be unpleasant. We were ushered individually into Mr. Stamp's office for interrogation. After each man went in and the door closed, the muffled sounds of raised voices and a body being slammed against walls and furniture could be heard. When the "interview" ended, the inmate was dragged or shoved by four guards to his cell. Bed and bedding were thrown from the room and the prisoner locked in. This was Southwestern Hospital's version of solitaire.

My turn came. When I went into the office, I was made to stand in front of Stamp's desk.

"Take off your glasses," one of the guards ordered. This was a bad sign. I knew somebody planned to hit me.

"I understand you are the ringleader of this whole mess," Stamp said.

"What?" I said, obviously aghast at such a charge.

Mr. Stamp sat erectly, his face flushed with the pleasure of power. The four guards stood nearby clutching their sticks. They seemed far less excited; probably they had planned on being home with their kids on Father's Day, not beating up people.

"What do you mean, *what?*" Stamp demanded.

"I don't even know what's happening," I stammered, lying with as much finesse as I could muster.

"You have the highest education of any of these animals. You must be the leader," Stamp said. "Were you planning on breaking out, Mr. Hester?"

"Oh, no, I love this place. And I think the world of you, Mr. Stamp," I said sarcastically.

"Hester, yore so fulla crap it ain't funny," Big John broke in.

"Maybe two weeks of solitaire will get you to tell the truth," Stamp said.

"Ah, hell, you might as well give me a month," I said defiantly, hate pulsing through my words.

"OK, you can have two months," he said. "Get him out of here."

I protested, but the guards quickly grabbed my arms and pushed me through the door. I didn't resist. We walked past the others awaiting interrogation and headed toward the wing where our sleeping cells were. One guard walked on either side grasping my arms, a third walked ahead, and a fourth followed. We stopped at the locked gate that served as an entrance to the cells. I looked through the grating and saw the beds and bedding littering the hall. The attendant in front of me rammed the key into the lock.

The metallic click of the key sent some type of signal deep inside of me, and I exploded with pent-up fury. I swung as hard and fast as I could and jolted the midsection of the guard on my left, breaking one of his ribs. I grabbed the one on my right around the neck, strangling him, and pulled myself off the floor—at the same time kicking the attendant to my front in the face, breaking his nose and shattering a cheekbone. The only one I couldn't attack, the man behind me, clubbed me, opening the skin on the back of my head.

I struggled on for a minute or so while none of them could subdue me long enough to hold me. Other guards joined them, several of them pounding me with their clubs. I only weighed 145 pounds, but I fought on, my strength coming from some mysterious, animal part of me.

The battle ended when I was clubbed into unconsciousness, my hair soaked with blood. The guards, panting and cursing, looked as bad as me, their starched white uniforms smeared with fresh blood—mine and theirs. They must have drugged me, because it was two days before I woke up.

When I roused, I realized I was naked, lying alone on a bare tile floor. My head ached, and I could feel the pain throbbing in bruises and welts all over my body. I tried to sit up but could only move a few inches in any direction. I realized I was bound by chains. My wrists were handcuffed behind my back, the cuffs linked to a heavy chain stretching from my waist to my feet. My ankles were shackled and hooked to the same chain.

The room was bare except for a pan of cold food and a bowl of water sitting on the floor near the door. I was hungry, but decided to wait for the next meal. In the evening an attendant exchanged a new pan of mushy, nondescript food for the previous one.

"Can you take these chains off while I eat?" I asked.

The guard looked at me blankly, then slammed the door without saying a word. No staff member ever spoke to me during my solitary confinement.

I crawled across the floor to the food. Like a dog I stuck my face in the dish, licking up bits of the brown, syrupy food with my tongue. It tasted terrible, as if two or three courses from a meal had been mashed together. No nurse or doctor came to look at my wounds. The gash in my head gradually healed, my skin mending the gap.

I soon learned the routine. At 6:00 A.M. and 6:00 P.M. a guard would open the door and silently lead me to a restroom. These two trips were my only daily visits to the toilet. Every three days the guard brought in another patient who led me, still in chains, to the shower. I stood under the cold stream for a few minutes while the patient rubbed me down with a coarse, brown soap. The chains never came off, and I remained naked.

Some days the poor food made me ill, and I developed diarrhea. I couldn't always wait until my six o'clock toilet visit, so I was forced to relieve myself in a corner of the small, hot cell. Since the room was only swept or mopped every three days when I was taken out for my shower, the odor from my sickness was overpowering and made me even more ill. Flies clustered on me and on the filth in the room. The guards would curse when they saw the mess. Flea powder was dusted on the floor after each mopping. The powder worked into my raw wounds, burning and itching.

After ten days, the walls of the cell seemed to be closing in, shrinking. All of the pain, terror, and humiliation of my life seemed to press in on me, threatening what sanity I had left. Finally, some barrier inside of me gave way, and I screamed—a piercing wail. Even though I still lay in chains, wallowing in my dirt, it seemed some part of me had died and I was free.

My mind and body started to heal, and to pass the time and to regain some self-worth, I began to exercise, hours on end, day after day. I discovered how to do modified sit-ups, did deep knee-bends by the hundreds, and walked. I paced off the room and calculated that 352 trips made a mile. Many days I walked ten miles, back and forth, my chains rattling behind me.

I disciplined myself to sleep during the day. Then I stayed awake at night, screaming and yelling for hours just to harass the guards and keep everyone on edge. I wanted the world to know Glenn Hester was alive, well, and tough. When my yelling became too disruptive, the guards would rush in, one of them pumping a shot of Thorazine into my behind. That would knock me out until the next morning.

Most of the time I thought of revenge, how I would kill my tormentors and escape.

After eight weeks, four guards came, opened the door, and snapped open my chains. When the handcuffs were opened, I found I could not raise my arms. My wrists were covered with sores from the rubbing of the metal bands. I had not shaved, and my eyes were sunken. I had lost ten pounds.

"You gotta cigarette?" I asked a guard, a gleaming smile

on my face. Inside, I felt I had won. I had proven I was stronger, tougher than any of them. I had survived alone. Nobody, I thought, would ever hurt me again.

"Hester, you even raise your hand or look cross-eyed at somebody, yore a dead man," Big John said. I believed him. I had heard rumors that John and two other guards recently had been charged with the murder of an inmate. Years later I learned this story was true when I read an old newspaper article.

The sores caused by the handcuffs were badly infected. The prison doctor gave me massive doses of penicillin for two weeks and they healed.

I was sent back to the maximum security ward where nothing had changed. Before long I was shining shoes for the guards again. I thirsted for revenge but soon realized that if I ever hoped to leave the place, I had to be cured. Being cured at Southwestern State meant being submissive and not hitting anybody. So I cured myself. I had my share of problems during the following months, but I never hit anybody. And I waited for the psychiatric evaluation. It never came, nor was I ever told how long I would have to stay. In the meantime, I became a model patient.

In November, six months after being admitted, without warning I was released.

I certainly was not a religious person, but as the deputy from Waynesboro drove me out the gate of Southwestern State Hospital, I prayed I would never again set eyes on its buildings, on its eight-foot-high, chain link fences topped with three strands of barbed wire.

I still remember that small room, the chains, and the sound of my screams piercing the night.

10. Glenn, I Love You

Waynesboro, Virginia, the 1960s

I was welcomed back to Waynesboro by Hank and Sarah, who were still numb and puzzled by my behavior and the subsequent imprisonment. I was glad to see them and quite excited. They were subdued—fearful, I suppose, of what I might do next to hurt and embarrass them.

My first week back I went before the judge again. He asked me some questions, revealing his ignorance of what had happened to me at Southwestern. While I had been away for the "evaluation," the judge had issued a court order to force Mother to send the letter giving Hank and Sarah proof of guardianship. The letter had arrived, and the judge order me to attend high school. He also assigned me to a probation officer.

Understandably, the staff and teachers at Waynesboro High were leery of my presence in the school. I was a seventeen-year-old ninth grader who had spent time in mental institutions and had a reputation for random violence against authority figures.

My first morning at school I met again with Mrs. Schneider, the guidance counselor. She began the wearying, thankless process of salvaging the tiny fragments of desire I still had for an education. In my early meetings with her, I acted tough and disinterested; but Mrs. Schneider was patient, seeing far more value in me than I did myself. The principal and teachers helped too, each one showing interest in me and helping me overcome my academic flaws. Many of them stayed after school-hours to help me fumble along with projects. To me the other students seemed young and unworldly, but I was accepted and even formed friendships.

Mrs. Schneider found me a job in the school print shop so I would have a few extra dollars to spend. When I needed encouragement, she always had a cheerful word or a bit of advice. My grades were poor the first semester, but the next term I made the honor roll.

For some months my life was unusually normal and tranquil. But my underlying fears and insecurity had only dipped beneath the surface, ready to emerge when pressures returned.

The school year ended. I worked at a frozen foods plant during summer vacation and was proud in the fall to buy my own school clothes and have some cash left over.

The fall semester started well, but I had a falling out with Hank and Sarah in November and had to find a new place to stay. Mrs. Schneider took me in. I lived with her and Mr. Schneider for a while until it became apparent I needed to be on my own.

I turned eighteen. At last I was legally free from the whims of my mother. Even the court washed its hands of me, releasing me immediately from the probation officer and other obligations when the morning of my eighteenth birthday dawned. It was as if this birthday had cured me magically of all my antisocial tendencies, and now I was emotionally fit to join adult society. I wasn't, of course, but the Virginia court system nonetheless had high hopes.

At Christmas break, 1966, I quit school and tried to join the U.S. Marines. I *had* to be a Marine, because I thought I was the toughest thing on two legs in the entire earth. But the Marine Corps found out about my stays in mental hospitals and turned me down. I was disappointed, but not long after my rejection, I received a draft notice.

One afternoon during Christmas vacation I walked to Denny's Music Shop, a popular meeting place for teenagers in downtown Waynesboro. I was listening to music, smoking a cigarette, and chatting with Denny when a girl walked in. She was slender, medium in height, and had long, brown hair that reached well down her back. Her face was fresh and clear, not masked by makeup. I was drawn to her immediately, though not in a sensual way, but rather because of her freshness and purity. She looked like a sweet flower blooming on a gray December afternoon.

The girl walked to the cash register and asked Denny to change a five-dollar bill. He did, and she slipped out the door, apparently unaware that I was in the store, my eyes riveted to the soft glow of her face.

"Denny," I said awefully, "who is that girl?"

"She's out of your league, Glenn," Denny said, laughing. "Her name is Mary Ann Heatwole. She's a Mennonite girl—works next door in the bookstore."

I did not believe *any* girl was out of my league. I flipped my cigarette on the floor, ground it out with my shoe, and headed for the small bookstore. I walked in, noting that the dream lady was behind the counter in the rear.

"May I help you," she called out, smiling.

"No, I'm just lookin'," I said, not quite certain yet of my strategy.

I drifted down the aisles, seeing quickly the store was filled with Bibles and religious books. These soon bored me, and since no other customers were in the shop, I walked to where the girl stood.

"Hi. What's your name?" I said, setting aside any further covering of my motives.

"Mary Ann," she answered, friendly but curious.

"My name is Glenn. I noticed you a minute ago in the music store. I couldn't help but notice how attractive you are. How would you like to go on a date?" I said this calmly; I was accustomed to being bold with girls.

Mary Ann stared at me a moment. Her mouth dropped open slightly, but no words came out. She flushed a bit, the extra color enhancing the healthy glow of her face.

"Well, ah, Glenn, you'll have to meet my father and ask him if I can date you," she said, her voice cracking a bit on the last words.

"What?" I said in disbelief. Girls I had known in the past never said such things. I didn't know what to say.

"I respect my parents. You will have to ask them," she continued with more confidence.

We talked for a few minutes. I learned she was nineteen, a few months older than I was. To my surprise, it seemed Mary Ann liked me, and she invited me to her home for supper the next Friday night.

If it's true that opposites attract, there could not have been a person more opposite from me than Mary Ann. She was sweet, fresh, naive, and pure. Here I was—bitter, worldly wise, and rotting from hate and unfulfilled revenge.

The next Friday at 6:00 P.M. I knocked on the door of Mary Ann's house. Her home was in the country, a neatly maintained house with a porch stretching across the entire front. I shuffled my feet nervously. It was dark and cold; my breath showed white in the moonlit air.

The door opened. Facing me was a tall, well-built man who invited me in properly, in a formal, cool way. Mary Ann entered the room, a wide smile on her face. She took my coat. Mr. Heatwole introduced me to his wife, an equally proper but somewhat reserved woman, and he and I sat down in the living room to talk before the meal. The women returned to duties in the kitchen.

I was uneasy, so I reached in my pocket for a cigarette, deftly tapping it on the pack before I lit up. About midway through my first delicious puff, I sensed by the pained look on Mr. Heatwole's face that I had done something wrong—what, I wasn't sure.

"You got an ashtray in the house?" I asked nervously, hiding my uneasiness with a huge, overdone smile.

There was no ashtray in the house. A small bowl was summoned from the kitchen.

Later I learned that Mennonites don't smoke. I had no idea that the term "Mennonite" referred to a type of religious faith. For all I knew, a Mennonite was something like a German or a Mexican.

The evening was off to a rocky start. I plunged on, though, eager to ingratiate myself to Mary Ann and her family. We visited as we ate supper, with Mary Ann's father conducting a gentle, but probing and effective interrogation.

"What do you do, Glenn?" he asked, handing me a platter nicely heaped with juicy ham.

"I just quit high school, Mr. Heatwole. I'm workin' on a construction job now."

Again, that pained expression flitted across his face.

"Tell us something about your family and background," Mr. Heatwole continued.

I gave them the whole story, deleting, of course, some of the more dramatic episodes—fights, being a mental patient, and the like. I was beginning to catch on to the ground rules of Mary Ann's family. I told them of the foster homes and some of the institutions, and how I had come to Virginia.

It was a struggle, but as I spoke I dropped all but the most crucial "hells," "damns," and other profanity from my vocabulary—an effort that to me reduced the impact but kept the pain in the Heatwoles' faces at an acceptable level. Mary Ann smiled encouragingly at times, although I sensed by the wideness in her eyes that she, too, was a bit taken aback by my story.

After supper the women went back to work in the kitchen while Mr. Heatwole and I returned to the living room to "talk." This development—being alone with my inquisitor again—made me very nervous, so I quickly lit another cigarette, coughing and blowing smoke furiously in all directions. As I had feared, now that we were alone the questioning became more pointed.

"Glenn, you seem to be a young man who is aware of the facts of life," he said, an intensely serious expression molding his entire face, seeming even to cause his ears to tighten.

I gulped and blew some more smoke. "I know my way around, sir," I said, amazing even myself with the extent of the understatement. I wondered if I should leave now before he learned more or stay longer and risk execution.

"Why do you want to take my daughter out?" he asked, his voice as cool and crisp as North Pole ice.

This is the clincher, I thought, my eyes beginning to swim and sweat breaking out under my arms. I took another long, deep puff on the cigarette, trying to form some words in my scrambled head that would abate Mr. Heatwole's fears.

"Ah, uh, I . . . she's, I find her very, ah, attractive. And—oh—she has a nice, uh, good personality," I said, relieved.

"Where do you plan to take Mary Ann?" he continued.

"To a movie, I guess," I replied, saying it more as a question than an answer.

Again the deep pain showed in his eyes. Later I learned Mennonites don't attend movies, either. Mr. Heatwole leaned back, looking first at me, then up at the ceiling; he was submerged in thought. I expected to be hung at dawn, or at best to get off with life imprisonment. After what seemed hours of heavy silence he spoke.

"Glenn, you can come visit our home anytime, but I don't think I want my daughter to go out with you—at least not now."

"Oh, that's fine, Mr. Heatwole," I said, sinking back in my chair. I wanted to light another cigarette to celebrate the inquisition's end, but decided against it.

All of us talked some more, then the evening was over. There was no good-night kiss, of course. But I did get to say good-bye to Mary Ann alone at the front door.

We began to see each other whenever possible. I would come to her house, and we would sit in the parlor and talk. Mr. and Mrs. Heatwole melted some, and occasionally I was permitted to meet Mary Ann in town after work. We would eat dinner at a restaurant, and then I would take her home—early. Mary Ann invited me to her church. I went because it meant I could sit near her, sneaking glances at her shiny brown hair and delicately colored face as the service droned on.

Mr. Heatwole began to tell me about his religion. He read parts of his big, worn Bible to me and told me I needed to be "born again" or "saved." I listened, but these words made no sense to me. Why did I need to be saved? I finally was on my own and had myself together.

One night in January I was hitchhiking home from Mary Ann's. The road was deserted, and it looked as though I would be doing more walking than riding. Then a set of car lights loomed on a hill behind me, and a minute later a car pulled over beside me.

"Where are you going?" the driver asked as I opened the car door. I told him and he motioned me in.

"I usually don't pick up hitchhikers," he said, "but I'll be happy to give you a lift. My name is Wayne Lawton. I'm a minister with the Free Methodist Church."

We talked as the car rolled along. I was pleased to be out of the cold.

The conversation gradually turned to religion. "Do you know Jesus, Glenn?" Wayne asked, smiling at me sincerely.

"Oh, yeah, I know all about Jesus," I answered, eager to establish some common ground. "My girl friend is a Mennonite, and she talks about him all the time."

We reached town where Wayne dropped me off. "Come to our church services sometime, Glenn," Wayne said, as I stepped out. I thanked him for the ride, hoping never to see him again. I liked him, but I wasn't planning on visiting churches as a hobby.

Several days later, on a frigid night when the temperature was near zero, I was hitchhiking home again from Mary Ann's. I had stayed with her later than planned, and with the road deserted, I wondered if any ride would come along. I walked briskly, trying to keep warm, but without gloves and wearing only a thin windbreaker, I grew colder each step.

After thirty minutes I saw the light from a roadside farmhouse. It was late, but I knew I must stop to warm myself or I might suffer frostbite. My ears were brittle and my fingers numb and painful. I rapped on the door. A man answered, flinging wide the door.

"Excuse me," I said. "I've been hitchin' and can't get a ride. I'm cold. Could I just stand in your doorway a few minutes and warm up?"

"Sure, come on in," the man boomed, welcoming me like a long-missing friend. "Here, stand by the stove."

I entered gratefully, shivering so severely my teeth chattered when I said "Thanks."

"My name's Henry Wingfield. Who are you?" the man said pleasantly, reaching to shake my hand vigorously. I introduced myself and told him I had been visiting my girl friend earlier in the evening.

"Where do you live, Glenn?" Henry asked.

When I told him, he quickly decided he would drive me into town. He put on his coat and went out to warm up his car.

In the meantime Henry's elderly mother had said hello and insisted on fixing a sandwich and bowl of soup for me.

"Oh, you look so cold, and you're such a young man," she said, patting me gently on the shoulder.

Henry came back in. The three of us visited several minutes until I finished eating. I said good-bye to Mrs. Wingfield, and Henry and I drove off.

In the car Henry and I visited some more. I related a bit of my past to him and mentioned I would be leaving soon to join the army. A mile from Waynesboro, Henry turned to me and said, "Glenn, do you know Jesus?"

I could not believe this. It seemed everywhere I turned somebody was trying to introduce me to God. I mumbled my answer, about the same thing I had told the preacher.

"Why don't you visit our church sometime—the Free Methodist Church," Henry said.

I remembered the name and knew he was talking about the same church where the man who had picked me up before was minister.

"Yeah, I'll try to come there sometime," I said. I thanked

him for the ride and said good night. *These Free Methodists sure are nice people,* I thought.

Two weeks later it was Mr. Heatwole who was after me again. "You need to know Jesus personally, Glenn, to be born again." Mary Ann, her parents, and I were sitting at the table after supper. I pondered what Mr. Heatwole had said. I wanted to make the Heatwoles happy, and I would do anything to keep seeing Mary Ann.

"What do you have to do to know Jesus?" I asked Mr. Heatwole. I was a little worried about what he might say, because I didn't care for weird religious practices.

"You just have to pray, Glenn, to confess your sins and ask God to forgive you. Jesus will be your savior then," Mary Ann's father said.

So I prayed, repeating a prayer word by word Mr. Heatwole spoke for me. I had no idea what was going on, but when it was over, the others were wet-eyed and grinning at me. I knew I finally had done something right—whatever it was I had done.

Mr. Heatwole talked for a few minutes about what was involved in being a Christian. "Now that you're a Christian, Glenn," he said, "will you still go into the army?"

I had received my draft notice and was to be inducted in March. "What do you mean?" I said, puzzled.

"Well, can't you tell the draft board that you're a Christian now and don't believe in killing—that you could never kill anyone?"

I stared at him blankly. One thing I tried not to do was lie, and saying such a thing would be a whopper. I was looking forward to the chance to practice killing people. I still had a long list of enemies I intended to murder when the time was right.

"No, I couldn't say I wouldn't kill somebody," I said finally. Mr. Heatwole disappointedly dropped the subject.

Only a few weeks of my civilian life remained, and Mary Ann and I saw each other nearly every day. I was in love with her, but I didn't know for sure how she felt about me.

Her twentieth birthday came. I used my entire two-week paycheck to buy her gifts—jewelry and a record player.

The night before I was to leave for basic training at Fort Bragg, North Carolina, Mary Ann and I stood at her door. I told her I would be gone at least three months, maybe more. "I'll think of you all the time and write," I said, my voice thickening.

"I'll write too, Glenn. Good night."

I left her, wondering when I would see her again and if there could be anyone who made me tremble inside like Mary Ann.

I was at the bus station at 5:00 the next morning, waiting with several draftees. The others and their parents and friends milled around, conversing infrequently, their choppy, awkward sentences broken by yawns. I was alone—until Mary Ann breezed into the station, her eyes radiant at the sight of me. My heart beat wildly, but I ached too; the bus would leave in fifteen minutes.

"Glenn, I have something for you," she said, handing me a small square package. I fumbled with the wrapping paper, uncovering a Bible with an olivewood cover. My name was engraved on the front.

"Oh, thank you," I said weakly. I had seen the Bible in her store once, and she knew I liked it. "Thanks, Mary Ann," I said again, my insides still quivering.

The bus pulled up and the passengers began to board. I put the Bible in a small athletic bag I was carrying and got in line. Mary Ann walked along beside me. When there was only one person between me and the bus door, Mary Ann suddenly faced me, threw her arms around my neck, and kissed me. As we held each other, I could feel her hot tears splashing down my neck.

"Glenn, I love you. Take care of yourself. Just keep the Lord in your heart."

We parted. I climbed the stairs, the door slammed, the bus rolled out. I waved to Mary Ann until the bus turned a corner. Slumped back in my seat, I raised my hand to wipe her tears from my neck. For the first time in years—*How*

*many had it been? At which institution had I stopped
crying?*—I felt my chin trembling and tears streaming
from my eyes.

"I love you, too," I whispered.

I stared out at the half-lit landscape. The bus engine
roared, fighting to climb the massive hills that encircle
Waynesboro, Virginia.

11. You'll Be a Dead Man

Dak To, South Vietnam, November, 1967

I awoke covered with sweat. A fly buzzed over my head, and the mid-afternoon sun was forcing light through the makeshift shades on my hootch. I looked at my watch— 2:00 P.M. I had slept seven hours, but was still tired, bone weary after nearly two months of working twelve-hour days without a break.

I lit a cigarette and grabbed a towel to wipe the sweat from my chest. The dog tags draped from my neck clinked when the towel passed. As I smoked, my mind still hazy from sleep, I began to think again of Mary Ann. Virginia was half a world away from the Republic of South Vietnam.

Three months earlier I had said good-bye to her for the second time. It had taken me six months to get back to Waynesboro after I left for basic training. The war in Vietnam had been hot, and even stateside leaves were hard to come by. I was destined for Vietnam duty, and the army shipped me from one training school to another without any break. I ended up being a meteorology technician, a fancy title for weatherman.

Finally, in September, I had returned to Waynesboro, eager to be near Mary Ann again. I had only seven days before I was to report for my flight to Vietnam. We had talked as we strolled through grassy fields. Fall was near, the temperature was cooling, the days sparkled. We had written often and had much to share. I was deeply in love and asked her to marry me. But Mary Ann was troubled. She and her parents opposed war. Mary Ann told me, finally, that she couldn't support the Vietnam war in any way, even by writing to me. This disappointed and hurt me, but I understood the depth of her feelings about religion.

"When I get back, we'll straighten things out," I told Mary Ann, my surface bravado covering internal fears. She looked at me and smiled, but did not speak.

I left for Vietnam, once again waving from the bus to Mary Ann. It was cold and raining. I ached inside, fearing I would never see her again. And I sensed that even if I did, the best times were behind us.

Vietnam was as bad as I had feared. Daytime temperatures in the dry season soared above one hundred degrees. In the rainy season, although it was not as hot, the humidity hovered near one hundred percent. My clothes always were damp from sweat. Bugs of all sizes and descriptions hummed through the air, dining day and night on whatever human flesh was available.

At Dak To I helped forecast weather for an artillery unit. Our firebase was huge, with over two thousand Americans living on it, but my unit of fourteen men was small. Ten of us were draftees or short-timers, the others were career men—"lifers."

The enemy harassed the base constantly with rockets, sending just enough each week to keep everybody on edge. The lifers bugged us, too, making the short-timers do all the work while they sat in their reinforced tents drinking and trading stories. The lifers made sure their names always were written on the roster sheets, but we seldom saw them on the job. We draftees drank constantly, too, although we tried to stay sober during our twelve-hour work shifts.

My unit's mission was to measure the wind and other factors that influenced the accuracy of our artillery guns. Based on our forecasts, we prepared and updated gun corrections around the clock. It was important and tension-filled duty. The combination of sticky weather, fatigue, danger, harassment from lifers, and heavy responsibilities pushed me too far. I became nervous, drinking too much and smoking pot heavily. I felt the reins on my impulsive temper slacking.

One day some of the artillery rounds from our firebase fell short in the jungle, killing one of our own infantrymen and injuring several others. The army brass started an investigation, and eventually my unit's records and gun calculations on the day of the incident were checked. Our team had been on duty when the tragedy occurred. The lifers got worried; they were supposed to be our supervisors and had their names on the duty rosters. They started hanging around, making us do picky odd jobs, trim our hair, and shine our boots. This was more than my thread-bare nerves could take.

"We're coverin' for you drunks," I yelled to one of the sergeants. "The army isn't going to lock just me up for killing those grunts. If I go down the tube, you're goin' too. I'll drag all of you into court."

The sergeant told me to shut up and get back to work.

My harassment from the lifers worsened after this out-burst. Some mornings at seven or eight I would just have fallen asleep after coming off duty. A sergeant would barge in and shake me awake. "Private Hester, you're supposed to be on duty," he'd growl.

"What do you mean? I just got off. I was up all night!"

"Oh . . . sorry about that," he'd say caustically.

Depression, which I had to fight off in the best of times, settled thickly on me, and I knew I had to get away for a vacation. I had been off duty only a few days in over four months in Vietnam, so one of the officers let me go to headquarters at Pleiku for a week.

While I was on "R and R," the Viet Cong unleashed the historic Tet offensive of 1967. The headquarters base where I was supposed to be resting was hit, too. No matter where I went, I could not get away from the war and my problems. Dead soldiers were scattered everywhere, and to top it off, an enlisted man working on a bulldozer near the end of an airstrip was hit one day by a low-flying airplane. His body was shredded into small pieces. I saw it happen.

This death and violence made me even more depressed. My nerves were raw; I sought out a doctor, and he gave me tranquilizers. Two nights later my mood went completely black. I hit bottom and no longer cared what happened to me. Desperate, I wanted only to feel better. I swallowed every tranquilizer the doctor had prescribed, twenty-five pills. I was not planning suicide; I just wanted some relief, and any reasoning ability I had left was hopelessly lost in the dismal, murky chambers of my mind.

After downing the pills I went for a walk. Crossing a parade field, I collapsed into unconsciousness. Some GIs stumbled onto me in the middle of the night. At the first aid station the medics found the empty pill bottle in my fatigue shirt pocket and pumped my stomach. I regained consciousness and was spared.

When my condition improved, I was shipped to the field hospital at Phan Rang for evaluation. The doctors there were surprised when I told them about my years in mental hospitals. The army had not checked out my past.

I was sent back to my unit, and the sergeants, knowing now about my mental history, started to set me up to their superiors as a crazy troublemaker who might have sabotaged records and caused the miscalculations in the artillery incident. I became even more tense and combative. The fuse on my violent temper was short and burning fast.

The commanding officer called me in for a talk. He decided I must be discharged from the military before I hurt somebody else or myself.

"I've looked through your records, Private Hester. You're going to fall apart over here," the captain said. "I don't think you've done anything wrong—yet, anyway—but your mental instability scares us."

At first the army wanted to give me a general discharge, but the brass later decided to let me go with a full honorable discharge. The U.S. Government didn't want me to get back on the street, blow somebody's head off, and then blame the army for my emotional instability.

So I packed my duffle bag, picked up my combat medals,

and flew home. My stay in the military had lasted less than twelve months. In March, 1968, I was back in Waynesboro looking for Mary Ann.

I never dated her again. My fears had come true; the relationship was finished. I asked my friends about her and learned she was away at college, engaged to marry another Mennonite. I didn't push to see her again. I thought of myself as a repulsive, filthy person—unclean. She was pure. I knew we were different, and I wasn't good enough for her. I loved her still, but I let the feelings die.

Finding a decent job proved difficult. I had a tenth-grade education and employers knew of my unsavory background. I finally had to return to the frozen foods plant as a laborer, a dirty, exhausting job.

At the plant I met a pretty girl. Her name was Alice, and I liked her. We started seeing each other after work, stopping for a drink or a sandwich.

Some months passed. Alice and I grew more serious and decided to marry. I found a minister, and we tied the knot. Although I still trembled on the brink of emotional collapse, I gave being a husband a try. My own upbringing had taught me little about responsible matrimony; and I was young, still thirsty for freedom and a wild time. Home life was rocky from the first day.

Two weeks after the wedding, I was driving toward Waynesboro in Alice's car, crawling up a steep mountain grade. I caught up with a dump truck hauling dirt. A breeze whipping down the pass was scattering dust from the truck's load and clouding my view, so I pulled into the center lane to pass. As I edged even with the truck, another vehicle, a sixteen-wheel semi, roared over the crest of the hill and sped toward me. The center lane was supposed to be used only by uphill traffic, but there was no time to fuss over who was breaking the rules. I braked, hoping to sneak back behind the dump truck, but its driver braked at the same time, keeping his vehicle even with mine. Desperately I pushed the accelerator to the floor, hoping to gun my car past the dump truck and out of the semi's path.

I didn't make it. The last thing I remember was being bounced around, hard. I didn't really wake up until the next morning at the Waynesboro hospital.

Two hitchhikers had seen the accident and later explained what they saw. When my car hit the semi, it went up in the air, hit some tree limbs above the highway, and flipped over. As the car turned in the air, I fell out the door and the car landed on top of me. The semi truck kept going, I was told, rumbling down the mountain. The driver of the dump truck stopped, walked back, and looked at my blood-covered body. Thinking I was dead, he shook his head, strode back to the truck, and drove on.

The hitchhikers ran up and pulled me out from under the car. I partially regained consciousness, and the two helped me to my feet. As I tried to stand unaided, a piercing pain shot through my back and I crumpled to the ground, again unconscious. My back was broken in two places. Had it been my time to die, I believe my life should have ended right there.

A roadside tavern was near the accident site. Its owner heard the racket, looked out the window, then immediately called an ambulance.

At the hospital I was later told my spinal cord had come dangerously near being severed. After hearing this from the doctor and seeing a picture of my demolished car in the newspaper, when I was alone again in my room I prayed haltingly: "Thank you, God."

My hospital stay lasted six weeks. Finally, after being fitted with a cumbersome back brace, I went home. There my shaky marriage rapidly neared collapse. I couldn't work, the bills mounted, Alice's car was wrecked. In the cramped trailer we snapped at each other.

In August, four months after the accident, I returned to work. But my weakened back prevented heavy lifting, and I had to quit. I found another job as a salesman in a paint store at a small shopping plaza, and finally was able to buy a secondhand car.

One afternoon at quitting time, I locked up the paint

store and walked to my car. I was slipping the key into the ignition when I heard a pop and then a crackling sound as the back window of the car shattered.

I jumped from the front seat, angry, yelling and cursing, wanting to find out who had broken the glass. When I ran to the back of the car, I saw a man standing about fifty feet away pointing a pistol at me. He fired, and I threw myself to the pavement, landing in a hard slide that ripped both of my pants' legs off at the knee.

Bullets snapped in the air above me. I looked up, finally realizing that shots were flying from two directions. I was in the middle of a gunfight; the man who had shot at me had just robbed a store in the mall and was exchanging fire with a security guard.

The robber jumped in a car and drove off, several police cars giving chase. Stunned, I picked myself up, hardly aware that my knees were bleeding and my pants were shredded. I got back in the car and inserted the key. As I raised my head I saw a clean round hole in the windshield, straight ahead, right between my eyes. My hands began to tremor. I slumped forward on the steering wheel, suddenly aware the bullet that shattered the back window had been fired from my front by the security guard—not from the robber in back—as I had leaned aside, fumbling with the key.

First the car wreck . . . and now this. For the second time in a year I knew I should be dead. I began to believe that somebody, somewhere, was looking out for me. "Thank you, God," I mumbled faintly.

The police caught the robber, and I helped identify him. The security guard denied shooting out my car window. I had to pay for it myself.

Although I believed God was watching over me, keeping me alive for some unfathomable reason, the way I lived didn't change. My marriage was gasping for life, and I drank heavily, hoping to forget my woes. My life had no foundation, and I was again unraveling emotionally. I was a mixture of child and old man—still hungry for basic love and security, yet jaded, hard, cruel, and unable to trust others or to contribute my share to a relationship.

Alice and I finally separated, then divorced. Our marriage had produced two children. Like my grandfather and father, I too had failed to give my children a permanent father. I quit my job and left town, drifting for months from place to place on the East Coast, from New York City to Miami.

Waynesboro was the closest thing to home I knew, so I went back. I hung around the city, seeing my kids whenever I could. I was bitter and sick, treading hard to stay above the surface of the sewer I was swimming in. Many months passed. I quit or was fired from one job after another and ended up driving a cab late at night, picking up drunks when the bars closed, fighting to get my fare money. I lived on the threshold of violence—selling moonshine out of my car trunk, sneaking around with other men's wives. After years of emotional slavery to fear and hate, my nerves were thin; my control was almost gone.

One afternoon in November, 1972, I was on my way to fill a prescription when a young woman stopped me on the street.

"Glenn, did you hear the news about Mary Ann?" she said.

"No, what happened?" I asked, noting that Marian, a cousin of my former girl friend, looked unusually grim.

"Oh, Glenn, it's so sad. Mary Ann was killed in a car accident in North Dakota."

"Oh, no. I'm so sorry."

I had not seen Mary Ann for five years but knew she had finished college, married, and moved with her husband to Minnesota. One morning, while driving on icy roads to her job as a music teacher across the border in North Dakota, she had crashed—dying instantly from a broken neck.

I mumbled a few more words of condolence to Marian, then hurried away, the tears brimming in my eyes.

Mary Ann's body was returned to Waynesboro. Wanting to give my respects, I cleaned myself up, dressed in my best clothes, and drove to the funeral home. The hostess ushered me into the chapel. Several people were there, talking quietly near the back. I walked to the open casket. There I saw again Mary Ann's long brown hair. Tears sliding down my cheeks, I touched her hand. "Thanks for everything, Mary Ann," I whispered.

I turned to leave, almost bumping into a tall, rugged young man who had walked up behind me. His face was tired and pale. I knew he had to be Mary Ann's husband.

"Hello," I said, "I am so sorry for your loss. I knew Mary Ann once. She was a wonderful person. My name is Glenn . . . Glenn Hester."

As an old boy friend I didn't expect much of a greeting from him. But a smile broke the sorrow on his face, and he shook my hand warmly.

"So you're Glenn. Mary Ann prayed for you constantly. She always hoped God would touch your life."

His words hit me hard. I began to cry again, overcome by the awareness that for the past few years there had been one person in the world who cared enough about me to mention my name to God. Mary Ann's husband consoled me, placing his arm around my shoulder. I hugged him, too.

Mary Ann's parents came over. They remembered me, and we visited a few minutes before I left.

The funeral was two days later, held in the Mennonite church. The service was jammed with people and was not sad but joyful. No one seemed bitter. The minister talked about how Mary Ann was now in heaven, a much better place. I believed it; Mary Ann had been a very good person, so very different from me.

The funeral impressed me. I envied the peace the people seemed to feel—even while facing the death of a lovely twenty-five-year-old woman. I left the church shaken, deeply troubled by the lack of peace, the desolation in my own life.

My routine continued. Severely depressed, I spent most

of my free time soaking up liquor in cheap bars, looking for some excitement, trying to forget my problems. On a Friday night in February, 1973, two of my friends, Willie and John, and I had about drained our fourth mixed drink at a bar where a rock band was playing. Three women walked in and sat down at a table not far from ours. We eyed them as they removed their coats, ordered drinks, and lit each other's cigarettes. It didn't appear they were waiting for anyone in particular.

"I'll take the blonde," I said to Willie and John. "You clowns can fight over what's left."

We walked wobbily to their table, introduced ourselves, then asked the girls to dance. I led the blonde, who I had learned was named Arlene White, to the small, crowded floor, and we began to dance. The band was blasting at high volume, so it was too noisy to talk. As we swayed to the music, we smiled at each other. Arlene looked to be about my age. I admired her shoulder-length blonde hair, and when we were close, I noticed her eyes were a light blue. They were like stunning, tiny blue magnets that threatened to tug my heart loose from its moorings.

We danced until the band's set ended three songs later. Back at the table we nursed our drinks. The bar was very crowded, and we had to shout to communicate above the roar.

"Are you married?" I yelled.

"Not at the moment," Arlene shouted back, laughing, teasing me with her eyes.

We danced some more, then found our coats, said goodbye to the others, and left. I drove Arlene to her apartment and spent the night.

Three weeks passed. Arlene and I saw each other now and then. We drank a lot, talked a little. When Arlene dropped her guard sometimes, sadness clouded her face and her eyes didn't shine. I knew she had problems, but I was so hopelessly buried in my own emotional refuse there was little I could do for her. We grasped at each other forlornly, hoping that together we might stay afloat awhile before life swallowed us up. It wasn't much of a relationship, but it was about all I had left.

In March, about 9:30 one Saturday night, Arlene got a message to me through the cab dispatcher. I was to come immediately to her apartment. I drove the cab quickly to where she lived, stopping near the front step of her building. Arlene bounded out the door, and to my surprise, came around the car to the driver's side and grabbed for the handle on the back door. I turned to my left, reached back, and pulled the inside handle.

"What're you sittin' back there for? What's up anyway?" I said, irritated.

She didn't answer, and as I slammed her door shut, someone roughly jerked open the front door on the passenger's side. I turned and saw a large, angry-looking man reaching for me. He slammed his hands around my neck and began to choke me. I swore angrily, but the words—muffled by his hands on my throat—came out a weak gurgle.

"I'll teach you to mess with my wife," the man snarled through clenched teeth.

I struggled, twisting and turning my body, trying to break his grip with my hands. He was frighteningly strong. His hands and fingers pinched my neck like huge pliers. Gasping for breath and beginning to faint, I slipped my hand into my jacket pocket. My fingers closed around the grip on my 25-caliber pistol. I slid the gun out and placed the small, cold barrel against the man's left eye. He froze.

"Brandon! He's got a gun!" Arlene screamed. "Glenn, don't shoot him!"

"Shut up!" I yelled. "Take your hands off of me, buddy, nice and easy," I ordered the man. He relaxed his grip and lowered his arms. "If you so much as blink, you're a goner."

We sat silently for some seconds. Light from a nearby street light shone through the windshield; I could see the man's face was pale, his eyes wild. I was still gasping for breath, and the muscles in my gun arm still twitched from the struggle. Arlene whimpered in the back seat, "I'm sorry . . . I'm sorry."

"I want you to know, Mr. Husband, that I don't like people puttin' their hands on my neck. If you can't keep your wife at home at night, that's your problem. But if you try a stunt like this again, your brains will be on the floor. Now, both of you, out of the car."

They left without a word. I drove off, still clenching the pistol in my right hand.

Arlene called me a few days later and admitted that she was married but had been separated for a year. Her husband had found out about the two of us and had forced her to set me up. I wanted to believe her story, so I did.

That same week we started seeing each other again. I put her husband out of my mind. Arlene told me he was a construction worker who lived alone in a cabin several miles from Waynesboro. He was working on a job in North Carolina and was gone most of the time.

Arlene neglected to tell me that after I had booted the two of them out of the cab, her husband had called the police and told them I had pulled a gun on him. The police asked him to come to the police station and file a charge, but he didn't.

The next Friday afternoon I picked up Arlene when she left work and took her to a bar for a drink. It was a warm, spring day, and I left my jacket—with the loaded pistol still in the pocket—locked in my car. I wasn't worried about Arlene's husband. Even if he were on his way home for the weekend, he wouldn't be back from Carolina until later in the evening.

We found a table, ordered our drinks, listened to the juke box, and watched the room fill as people came in to celebrate the end of the week. We sat close together, holding hands, our backs to the entrance. We didn't see Arlene's husband and two of his friends come in. Suddenly, I felt hands grab my shoulders and lift me from the chair.

After his companions had me restrained, White confronted Arlene. "I warned you, Arlene. I'm not putting up with this! You're still my wife!" he yelled, slapping her face.

The chatter and movement in the small bar diminished. Heads turned. Soon there was a tense silence, except for the music blasting from the juke box.

"Get him out of here. I'll take care of her," Arlene's husband yelled, motioning for his two friends to dispose of me.

The two tanned, muscular men strong-armed me through the door. I wanted to fight, but I didn't have even a pocket knife on me, and the two were big. Outside they slammed me against the brick front of the bar. One of them grasped my shirt and twisted it tight against my neck.

"You're lucky it's still daylight and there are witnesses, or we'd beat the crap out of you," he said. "You better just move out of here and keep your yellow, stinking hands off Brandon's wife. If you ever go near her again, you'll be a dead man."

As he let go of me, he pushed me away and ripped the top of my shirt. This amused them, and they both laughed.

I cursed them and ran away, intending to get the pistol and kill them and Brandon, too. But as I reached my car, a police cruiser squealed to a stop in front of the bar. Two policemen ran inside. I quickly slipped into my car and drove away.

The more I thought of this public humiliation, the more I longed for revenge. Irrationally, I thought all of my problems would ease and the dank depression gripping me would lift if Brandon White were dead. I learned where White lived and twice drove to his cabin hoping to catch him alone. Both times his place was deserted.

I wasn't seeing Arlene anymore, and I missed her. I became obsessed with getting revenge on White. Finally, disgusted because I could not confront White in person, I wrote him a note, telling him that when he had pulled his little scene at the bar, he had signed his own death warrant. No one who had roughed up Glenn Hester twice could expect to go on living.

I didn't know it at the time, but the moment I dropped that card in a mailbox, I had committed a felony: extortion through the mail. I had threatened to kill someone.

When White received my letter he panicked and called the police again. This time he went to the station and showed the detectives the note. Since I now had committed a federal offense, the FBI took the case. Federal agents began to investigate me and subtly keep track of my activities.

White didn't respond to my note, so finally in frustration, one night in May I reached him by telephone.

"Mr. White, this is Glenn Hester again. Why don't you meet me out in the woods? We'll settle this thing man to man. If you really want to keep Arlene, why won't you fight me for her? Do you need a gun to fight with? I'll loan you one."

White cursed me and hung up.

The next morning two FBI agents knocked on my door. They read me my rights and told me White had initiated a felony charge against me. The agents drove me to their office in Charlottesville. I told them what I had done, in the process admitting my guilt. They brought me back home.

The grand jury met, reviewed the case, and indicted me. A probation officer was sent to interview me before the trial to learn for the court whether a prison sentence or probation would be more appropriate. After the man heard of my problems and frequent encounters with the police, he casually said: "You'll probably get five years in prison this time."

I was stunned. I hadn't *done* anything. In my twisted mind it was White who was causing the problems.

My anger against White, the system, and myself grew. And with it grew my dulling, disabling depression. I wanted to lash out, to perform some final act of justice against White. But I didn't know what to do.

The last week of June I went on a drinking spree, in the process losing my job as a management trainee at a fast-food restaurant. I had been staying again with Aunt

Sarah—she liked having company since Uncle Hank had died the year before. I didn't want her to see me drunk, so I had crashed at Willie and John's place for several days. I stumbled around their house, so emotionally broken I would begin to cry for no reason, sobbing like an abandoned child.

On Saturday night, June 30, I was slumped in the living room, weak from the ravages of alcohol. I watched a television program where a man killed someone and received a ten-year term. He was paroled and set free after serving six years.

Why not go ahead and kill White? I thought. *I can shoot him and end up with six years. What's one more stinking year in jail matter when I can get even?*

I loaded my car with guns and drove into the sweet smelling night, headed for White's cabin in the country. I was quite sure he would be there or show up before long. As I drove I began to cry uncontrollably. Ahead on the interstate highway I saw the green exit sign, the road leading to Brandon White's.

12. No Longer Alone

Waynesboro, Virginia, July 1, 1973

The tears, those blasted, burning tears, dripped down my cheeks, blinding me. Gripping the steering wheel with my left hand, I pushed the stained eyeglasses to my forehead, rubbing the wetness from my eyes with the sleeve of my undershirt. Without lenses I was nearly blind. The car swerved back and forth across the center line, the tires squealing until the glasses were again in place and my steering true.

Thoughts gushed like a swollen stream through the twisted channels of my mind: *I've got to kill Brandon White. He's humiliated me. He's forcing Arlene to stay away from me. He's filth. How can I lure him out of his cabin? It's late—must be after midnight—White might be in bed . . .*

"This is stupid—what's wrong with me—I really don't want to kill this guy!" I yelled, pounding my fist on the wheel. The sound of my voice echoed in the car, hurting my ears.

"Oh God, I need help. I'm a mess . . ." The tears bulged in my eyes again, and I sobbed. The road blurred. The car swung widely as I struggled to avoid a skid. I was trembling, my arms and hands felt weak. A sickness bubbled in my stomach.

I am afraid. The thought clambered triumphantly to the top of the garbage heaped in my mind. *I'M AFRAID.*

I hate the fear. Why do I need to kill Brandon White to prove I'm not afraid, to prove I'm not weak?

The highway, which wound through green-wooded valleys now dark and mysterious, was nearly deserted. A car approached ahead, and its headlights dimmed. The flash of the light jarred me; I realized suddenly that the exit road leading to Brandon White's cabin was ten miles behind me.

"You missed the exit, you stupid . . ." I muttered. I considered turning around but drove on, somewhat relieved. I rounded a curve and saw ahead the sky glowing with dots of light. *I'm almost to Charlottesville. Now what?*

My clothes were grimy and reeked of sweat; I knew I couldn't join the all-night party I usually attended on Saturdays. Anxiety gripped me again, and the ache in my forehead throbbed. A wave of warmth spread up my face, and my palms moistened. I could feel fear lurking, poised in the darkness of my mind.

A lighted green sign announced a Charlottesville exit. I steered down the ramp and stopped at the bottom. To the right, about a quarter of a mile away, stood a service station—closed. But nearby was a phone booth, its white light piercing the darkness like a beacon. I drove to the light and switched off the engine.

Cars passed infrequently on the street behind me, breaking the stillness. Staring at the booth I was unsure about what to do next. Minutes passed. *Should I call up White, make him lose some sleep? Maybe I could call someone at the party.*

I stepped from the car and slammed the door. The heavy, warm evening air soothed me. The night insects were in chorus, their voices grating with the clamor in my head. In the phone booth I wrestled some change from the pocket of my jeans—a quarter and some pennies. I dropped the large coin into the slot and dialed zero.

"Operator. May I help you?" a woman answered. She waited expectantly. I didn't know what to say.

"Hello? May I help you?" she repeated a bit louder.

I cleared my throat. "Yes. Right now I'm a desperate person. I need some help. I need to talk to somebody."

The woman paused, befuddled.

"Ah, sir, could I perhaps place a call to someone for you?" the operator said finally.

"I don't have nobody to call. I just need to talk to somebody. Can you help me?" My words surprised and irritated me. *Why am I talking to this woman like this? I sound weak.*

"Oh! There is a place, er, let me look here. . ." I heard pages in a directory rustling in the background. "These people counsel over the phone. Yes, here it is, it's called The Bridge. The number is—" she rattled it off.

I did not answer.

"Sir? Did you hear me?"

"Oh, yeah, what's the number again?"

"Why don't I dial it for you."

She did. I heard the call ring once . . . twice . . . three times.

"Hello. This is The Bridge. May I help you?" said a man whose voice had a youthful ring. The operator clicked out, happy, no doubt, to move along to the next call.

"Yeah, I need to talk to somebody right now. My name is Glenn. I'm upset, very upset about what's happening in my life."

"Where are you now, Glenn?"

I told him. He explained that The Bridge was just a mile away and gave me the address and directions.

"I'll be right over. Good-bye." I hung up and climbed into the car, repeating the address out loud so I wouldn't forget.

As I turned the car onto the street I thought, *What kind of stupidity are you getting into now, Hester?* No one was moving about. I passed a flashing bank sign: It read: 78° / 1:30 A.M.

I found The Bridge easily—an older house, its porch glowing from a yellow light. I stopped in front, switched off the headlights, and with the car idling, carefully eyed the house. Above the doorway was a plywood sign cut and painted so that it resembled a bridge. I was embarrassed and scared and wanted to leave. But inside the house a lamp burned, its light warm and inviting.

I'm tired. I've no place to go. I want to talk. I might as well give it a try. I turned off the engine, walked to the door, and knocked. Waiting for someone to answer I again realized my body smelled and my clothes were grimy. I rubbed my hand across my face; the whiskers were stubby and sharp. The door opened. Facing me was a tanned, barefoot young man wearing ragged jeans and a University of Virginia sweatshirt. His hair hung well over his ears. He looked to be about twenty and was smiling broadly, seemingly unconcerned with my odor and dirty clothes.

"I called," I said, feeling awkward.

"You must be Glenn. Come in." The man pushed open the screen door with one hand and firmly shook my hand with the other. "My name is Paul."

I entered a living room furnished with a couch, several chairs, and scattered lamps. The furniture was worn but clean. I sat down, looking the room over carefully.

"Would you like a cup of coffee, Glenn?" Paul asked.

"Sure . . . thanks."

Paul left. I looked some more. Across the room stood a table with two phones, a note pad, pen, and Bible perched on top. A clock and two posters of nature scenes hung on the wall facing me. I noted the time: 1:40.

"Here's your coffee, Glenn—and some doughnuts. I thought you might be hungry," Paul said as he returned.

He sat down across from me, settling comfortably in a stuffed chair. I sipped the coffee and took several bites of a stale doughnut. I was hungry, so it tasted good. But I still didn't have the nerve to discuss why I had come. I avoided Paul's eyes by staring at the floor.

"Well, Glenn, it sounded like you were having some trouble. Do you want to talk about it?" Paul said finally. He smiled again and interlaced his fingers behind his head.

The food and coffee had revived me, and I felt more like talking. "I was thinking of killing this creep named Brandon White tonight, but I missed the turn on the interstate and ended up here."

Paul nodded but said nothing. I belched, licking the icing from my fingers, and reached for another doughnut.

"This guy humiliated me in public and tried to rough me up twice," I went on. "His wife don't want him no more. She

wants me. But he's got her so scared she won't see me. I
don't know what to do about it, and I may have to go to
prison because I threatened to blow him away."

Still no word came from Paul.

"I'm very nervous now and sick of the crap in my life. I've
been drinkin' . . ." My voice trailed off. I looked at Paul and
thought, *Is this really happening? I'm here spilling my guts
to some "Mr. Clean" stranger, some kid, in the middle of the
night?*

"Tell me some more about yourself, Glenn," Paul coaxed.

I did want to talk. I started at the beginning with Mother
leaving me, the foster care, the abuse. The names, places,
and episodes of my life rolled from my tongue. In a perverse
way the disgusting story still impressed me, even though
I'd told it a hundred times—to social workers, psychiatrists, lawyers, judges, and friends. This was a first,
though, telling it to some kid in the dead of night.

Paul listened intently, showing no alarm as I described
the beatings, the insane asylums, the sexual escapades, the
booze running, the continual violence. *Does he believe me?* I
wondered.

After forty-five minutes, pausing only for yawns and
more coffee, I finished. "So I'm strung out tonight. I don't
know what to do with this guy White."

Paul thought for a while, looking first at me then at the
floor.

"Glenn, you've told me about the things people have
done to hurt you, but do you see what you're doing to yourself? You've gotten yourself in a spot where you don't have
control over your life."

"Yeah, I see that. I would like more control, but . . ."

Paul smiled again. "Have you ever thought about God?"

I shifted uneasily in the chair, not sure what to say.
"Sure, I've thought about God. I've talked to him many
times. But he doesn't seem to listen to me. I'm filth—I'm
not good enough for God. He wants decent people who go to
church all the time, like Mary Ann I told you about. He
don't want me. I'm a bum."

Paul looked at me kindly. Then he leaned forward, bracing his elbows on his knees. Only four feet separated us, and my anxiety soared. The God-talk was irritating me.

"It seems you are always giving God your problems, Glenn. Are you willing to give God your *life?*"

I didn't like what he had said; it made me mad. *This is getting too religious,* I thought.

"Like I said, man. God don't want me. I stink. God wants clean, good people—like you."

"No, God takes what he can get. If you're willing to give your life to God, he can change you, make you new. He loves you. You're important to him."

By this time I was very tired and not in the mood to have some kid stuffing religion down my throat. "I need to be going," I said, standing abruptly. "Thanks for the coffee and doughnuts."

"You're welcome, Glenn. Come back and see us any time."

I left. I drove away, slowly gliding through the dead streets. Nothing was moving except the same flashing bank sign: 76° / 4:10 A.M.

Still not sure where to go, I headed west to Waynesboro. I was disgusted with Paul and his give-it-all-to-God speech. *I won't do anything about White tonight,* I decided; *I'm too tired. I would just foul it up.*

The car hummed through the stillness. I thought again of Paul's words, and an argument erupted in my mind . . . *This guy says God loves me, that God is concerned with me! . . . What a joke! Where was God when I was left behind by Mother or beaten to a pulp at Southwestern? When's the last time God stopped by to be a buddy, putting his arm around my shoulder?*

What if it's true, that God does care for me and not just the good people? . . . No, God creates us, winds us up, turns us loose. He doesn't care. My life's been screwed up, and now I'm paying for it.

I crested a hill and saw the lights of Waynesboro ahead. I

wanted to go somewhere and sleep, but I couldn't shake my mind off what Paul had told me about God. An eerie feeling gripped me. I sensed within my tangled mind something unusual; I felt as though I were being called, drawn toward something good, something warm, something bright, something clean. The something felt like love.

I shook my head vigorously. "Are you crackin' up, Hester?" I asked aloud. At Waynesboro I exited. Without stopping I crossed over the bridge above the interstate, turned left, and headed east again to Charlottesville, to The Bridge. I knew I had to learn more; I had to find out if God really cared for me; I had to talk to Paul.

A half hour later in Charlottesville I again passed the familiar blinking bank sign: 76° / 4:57 A.M. I had driven ninety miles since starting out to kill Brandon White hours ago.

The lights were out at The Bridge. I knocked timidly on the door. There was no answer. I knocked again, more sharply. Still no answer. *He must be sleeping. I have to talk to this guy some more. I'll wait.*

I collapsed on the porch, leaning my back against the front door. Weak with fatigue, I drew my arms around me, shut my eyes, and fell asleep.

I was awakened by the sound of a lock clicking. Then I raised my head and my shoulders started to slide. Someone was opening the door. Still numb from sleep, I jerked myself to a sitting position. Through bleary eyes I saw that the sun was up.

"Glenn! I thought you went home!" It was Paul.

Still trying to clear my head, I said thickly, "I did. But I wanted to talk some more. When I got back nobody answered the door."

"Well, come on in . . . how about some breakfast? We'll be eating in a few minutes. Come on," Paul said. He looked sleepy, too.

Inside, young women and men were scurrying back and forth carrying platters heaped with food. I was stone sober now, and my stomach groaned as I sniffed the inviting odors of hot food and freshly brewed coffee. Paul led me into the living room. The wall clock read 8:35.

"Would you like to wash up?" Paul asked as we walked toward the dining room. I nodded.

In the bathroom, while splashing water on my face, I saw in the mirror how repulsive I was. My hair was stringy, darkened from sweat. The eyes were bloodshot and baggy, and a five-day growth of whiskers smudged my face. The undershirt I had put on three mornings ago was torn and soiled, smelling potently of dried sweat. My jeans were spotted with grease. I looked like a back alley wino; only a bottle in a brown paper sack was missing. I searched my pockets in vain for a comb. Since there was nothing I could do to improve my appearance, I dried my face and hands and left.

In the dining area eight people sat at a long table, all of them talking excitedly, laughing, enjoying the morning. They looked rested, and no one seemed hung over from a party. *What kind of weirdos are these? This is Sunday morning.*

The table was covered with food: scrambled eggs, fried potatoes, grits, ham, toast, orange juice, doughnuts, milk, and coffee.

Paul, who was standing beside me, whistled loudly to get the attention of the others. "Y'all listen up," he said. The fresh, smiling faces turned expectantly my way. "This is Glenn—ah—Hesten—*Hester*. He's from Waynesboro and stopped by last night."

"Hello! . . . Hi! . . . How ya doing!" the greetings rang out.

I smiled, mumbled a hello, and quickly sat down. I was embarrassed by the way I looked.

A young man stood and prayed a blessing, after which everyone except me murmured "Amen."

The food was passed. My hands shook as I filled my plate. I ate ravenously—three helpings—talking little as I hurriedly shoveled the food into my mouth. The uncontrollable way I was eating made me self-conscious too, but I was so hungry I really didn't care what the others thought.

Soon the serving platters were empty and the meal ended, but I was still hungry. While the others stacked and cleared dishes, I nursed my coffee.

"Glenn, we are getting ready to go to church. Do you want to go with us?" It was Paul again.

"Are you kiddin'? I look like a bum. No church is gonna let me in," I said, hoping he would agree with me. I didn't care much for churches.

"Hey, don't worry about how you look; at this church people don't care."

"No thanks. I'm not interested," I said sharply. I still wanted more food and was grumpy from a lack of sleep. I just wanted to lie down somewhere. The thought of sitting through some boring church service was more than I could handle.

Persistent Paul tried one more angle, and it worked: "We have a nice dinner after church. There's plenty to eat. You could join us . . ."

"OK, I'll go," I answered, allowing my stomach to decide for me.

The others locked the house, and we loaded into the cars. It was only 9:30, but the sun was high and no breeze disrupted the smothering heat. Paul and another young man, Gary, offered to ride with me. The seats were littered with empty beer cans, girlie magazines, and other trash. My riders cleared spots to sit and climbed in.

The car had no air conditioning, and I began to sweat. We opened all of the windows. As I accelerated and headed from town, Paul and Gary spoke loudly, trying to be heard above the roar of the wind and the car's engine.

After yelling out directions, Paul said, "Glenn, we go to a church that's in the mountains. It's a place called Oakleigh." I nodded my head and smiled weakly. I didn't care if their church was in a graveyard. I regretted my decision to come, but I did want another meal.

After winding through several wooded valleys and hills, we turned into a narrow lane. A short distance further we reached a clearing, dominated by a massive stone and brick house, a mansion. Cars were parked helter-skelter on the landscaped grounds.

"Where's the church?" I asked.

"This is it. We meet inside the house," Gary answered.

We parked and Paul and Gary hurriedly left the car. The service had begun, and as the others rushed toward the building, I nearly had to sprint to keep up. We climbed the front steps, crossed a wide veranda, and entered through eight-foot-high, solid wood doors.

As I stepped across the threshold, a wave of cool air hit my face. This perked me up; I was glad to leave the muggy heat behind. At the far end of the long, high-ceilinged room where I stood, a cluster of people were singing a rousing song.

Paul and Gary walked in that direction. I hung back, warily standing near the doorway. The beauty of the room delighted me. Ceiling-to-floor bay windows filled one entire wall. The morning sun streamed through the glass, spotlighting the deep, royal blue carpeting. The crystal tips of two glittering chandeliers sparkled in the light. Expensive-looking pieces of dark wood furniture and several towering brass floor lamps had been pushed aside to make room for about twenty short rows of metal folding chairs.

The chairs were empty, though; everyone but me was up front singing. Some of them clapped in rhythm, raising their hands joyfully.

I liked the cool and comfortable room. But the church service puzzled me. I decided to sit down as far to the back as possible, next to the door. I wanted to be near the exit in case I needed to escape.

The singing went on. The melodies were appealing and the rhythms fast. I noticed several people had their arms around each other.

This is a strange church, unlike the dark, cold sanc-

tuaries of some churches I've visited. Everyone seems to be enjoying this . . . they're smiling. It looks like a party.

Along the wall opposite the bay windows stood two long tables heaped with food. Casserole dishes, desserts, breads, salads, vegetables, and relishes. My mouth watered. I hoped the service would end soon, but knowing it couldn't be too long before dinner made me more patient. I leaned back and stretched my legs under the chair in front of me. *Maybe I can catch a nap.*

"Glenn, why don't you go up to the front and apologize to God for everything you've done to him. Ask him to forgive you for the way you've led your life," someone who was sitting behind me said.

I jumped. I hadn't seen anyone slip in after me. My face flushed with anger. I didn't like strangers—or anybody for that matter—telling me what to do. Impulsively I snapped: "Me apologize to God? God owes me an apology for sticking me with the life I've had!"

I sat up straight and glanced behind my shoulder, anxious to see who was blabbing in my ear about God. There was no one behind me. I turned sideways, then completely around. I was facing a blank wall. There were no chairs behind mine; I was sitting in the back row.

My heart began to pound and sweat broke out on my brow. My breathing speeded up. I was scared. *What's happening to me? I heard a voice. Am I cracking up?*

I looked to the front. The others were still singing, their voices in chorus filling the room. No one was looking my way.

I've got to get out of here! I leaped up and strode three steps to the doors, which were closed. Shaking, I grasped the door knob. I wanted to run away, but somehow I couldn't force myself to move. My feet seemed leaden, anchored to the floor. My heart was leaping in my chest, and I felt weak from terror.

I stood motionless for a few moments, my mind crippled by indecision. Then it became clear what I needed to do: *I must join the others.*

I walked slowly to the front. About forty people, young and old, black and white, were grouped in a half circle, three rows deep. They were still singing. A young man, who was casually dressed and holding a songbook, faced them leading the song. There was a break in the circle, a passageway in front of me. I walked through it until I stood before the leader. I had begun to cry, just as I had in the car the night before, the tears splashing uncontrollably from my eyes, dripping through the stubble on my cheeks. Desperate with fear, longing for some final solution to my pain, I stepped near the song leader and put my arms around him.

"I need help. I'm scared," I whispered hoarsely, a sob cracking in my throat.

The young man was startled momentarily, then with a compassionate look placed an arm around me. Suddenly, I realized what I had done. *What am I doing putting my arms around this guy? They'll think I'm gay.* Angrily, I pushed him away. "Don't touch me. Don't *ever* touch me, again," I snarled.

Now the song leader was really confused. He stepped back from me. Oddly, the others went on singing, although several were eyeing me curiously.

"Glenn, I want you to get down on your hands and knees. I want you to beg for your life." It was the voice again behind me, the one I had heard in the back of the room.

I swung around and faced the group, shaking my right fist above my head. "I don't get down on my hands and knees for anybody!" I thought I had screamed these words, but no one seemed to have heard me.

My mind began to race, thoughts tumbling in a vicious torrent. I remembered the guards at Southwestern State Hospital yelling at me, making me crawl. *Shine my shoes, boy!* I was furious. I would not kneel in this crazy church. I would not crawl for anybody.

The singing still hadn't stopped. *Am I going mad?*

Suddenly, I was knocked to the floor, so sharply my glasses flew from my face and tumbled across the rug.

Without them my vision blurred. I was confused. I didn't know who or what had flattened me. I looked up. Near me, among those who were still singing, I saw a few people I knew from high school. They were looking at me, and I could tell they recognized me. One of them whispered, "That's Glenn Hester. I remember him from high school. He's always in trouble!"

I cowered and dropped my head in shame. I was embarrassed that someone who knew me, the toughest guy on two legs, should see me groveling on the floor in a church service.

"Glenn." It was the voice again. "I love you very much. Unless you give me your life, you're going to die. I want you to apologize. I love you . . . I love you . . ."

"No, I will not apologize to anyone!"

Time seemed to slow, then stop. My life passed in review, the faces, events, and places unrolling from my memory. I could tell it definitely was my life I was seeing, but my viewpoint had changed. Now I was seeing not what others had done to me, but what I had done to them.

I saw myself teasing my brother, enticing him to fight . . . talking back to Mother . . . swearing at the social worker . . . flattening the boy's nose with the frying pan at Pinewood . . . hitting Mother in the face . . . knocking out the guard at Spofford . . . beating up Nurse Peoples at the mental hospital . . . running away . . . knifing Charles Treney . . . shooting out windshields with the BB gun . . . threatening to kill Brandon White—I saw it all in a few moments. All the anger, all the lust for revenge, all the hate.

The replay of my life as I'd known it ended, but there was one more horrifying scene: I saw myself leaving Oakleigh and nothing had changed about me; I was a desperate man filled with fear and violent hate . . . Later I had assembled my guns. I was barricaded, alone, shooting people, crying, screaming for revenge as the shells exploded. My victims, people I did not know, were dying, and then the sirens wailed and the police came. They crouched behind barriers, pointing their rifles at me. Then their bullets ripped my body. I was silent. Dead.

The playback ended. Time began again. I was kneeling on the floor at Oakleigh. A decision had to be made.

"I don't want to die . . . Lord, yes, Lord Jesus, forgive me, Lord," I said, over and over, my tears of regret and shame dropping to the floor. The weight and filth left me. My lips fell silent. At last I was free. At last I was no longer alone.

13. I Love You, Lord

Charlottesville, Virginia, July 1, 1973

On my knees that sun-drenched morning at Oakleigh, I became a Christian—a follower of Jesus Christ.

After I finished my prayer and stood up, one of the church's leaders asked me to explain who I was and what had happened. I spoke quietly for a minute or two, my voice cracking, explaining a bit of my past and the pain and desperation in my life. I told them how someone had called out to me, only minutes earlier, asking me in an intimate way to let him control my life.

I smiled. Everyone smiled back. I sat down. The group gathered in a circle, some of them placing their hands on me. "Thank you, Lord, for Glenn," one of them prayed.

After the service ended, person after person came up to me, shook my hand, and hugged me. Most had tears in their eyes. "I'm so happy the Lord found you," an older woman said. I could not stop smiling. I wasn't sure yet what had happened, but instead of being filled with anxiety and pain, I felt warm, strong, and clean inside.

My dirty clothes and unwashed body made me self-conscious, but the people at the church didn't seem to care. Before long I surrendered myself to the joy. Dinner time came. My excitement postponed my hunger, and I ate only one helping. At the table, on all sides of me, people introduced themselves and asked me questions. It seemed already they really cared about me.

Paul came over. "Glenn," he said, putting his arm around my shoulder, "I'm your brother now; you're in the family of God—you've been *adopted!*" Before the afternoon ended, I knew I had many brothers and sisters who loved having me in the family.

At 5:00 P.M., after talking almost nonstop all afternoon, I felt tired and decided to leave. Stopping on the veranda on the way to the car, again I was hugged by several of my new brothers and sisters.

"Come back soon, Glenn," said Don, one of the people who lived full-time at Oakleigh. "We have Bible studies and prayer every night."

"I'll be back," I answered. I knew that this time I was telling the truth.

I crawled into my car and waved as I drove off. The interior was hot, so I halted to roll down the windows. I started off again, rushing down the mountainside and through the green valleys. I gripped the wheel hard, threw my head back, and whooped with delight. The earth seemed new and fresh; I inhaled deeply, savoring the delicate fragrances of summer.

"I haven't had a cigarette since this morning!" I said aloud, amazed. The afternoon had passed so quickly with talk and laughter I had forgotten to smoke. Normally I used two packs a day. I laughed, waving my left arm out the window. "I don't even want a smoke now," I yelled.

I drove on into Charlottesville, stopped at a men's clothing store in a shopping mall, and bought a new shirt and pair of pants. Drained of energy, I decided to spend the night in a hotel. After checking in, I bought a razor, some blades, and shaving cream from a vending machine. In the room I showered and shaved. I crawled into bed at about seven and reflected on the day, on all that had taken place since Paul had found me eleven hours earlier on The Bridge's front porch. I wondered if this was just another high, and if the pain and fear would be back in the morning. But as sleep pulled me under, all I could do was smile and whisper over and over, "Thank you, Lord, thank you."

When I opened my eyes the next morning I was surprised to see bright sunlight slanting through the shades. I lay silent a few minutes, finding it unusually difficult to wake myself. Having lived with heavy anxiety for so long, I was unaccustomed to waking from deep sleep. I slipped my eyeglasses on and looked at the clock on the nightstand. It read 9:00 A.M. I stared in disbelief at the dial. *Could I have slept that long without waking?*

Normally I rested fitfully, waking two or three times before morning, craving a cigarette. It had been years since I had stayed asleep for an entire night. Something had changed yesterday. I felt fresh and full of energy.

"I love you, Lord!" I said aloud.

After another shower and shave, I put on my clean clothes. The hotel had a restaurant, and I ate a huge breakfast. Afterwards I checked out and drove out of town, west to Waynesboro.

"Where do you want me to go, Lord?" I prayed as I drove along. I passed by the exit to Brandon White's cabin. No longer wanting to harm him, I was sobered by the thought of how close I had come to killing him just thirty-six hours before. I drove past Waynesboro, too, still excited and not ready to come back down to earth.

About noon I arrived in Staunton, a small city about fifteen miles west of Waynesboro. I wandered through the city's streets for a few minutes, finally pulling over and parking in front of some specialty shops. Turning off the ignition, I glanced to my right. My eyes focused on a sign— "Bob's Gun Shop." I remembered the guns in the trunk, knowing instantly what the Lord wanted. I needed to get rid of those guns.

I unlocked the trunk and gathered the shotguns, rifles, and pistols in my arms. I hauled them inside, setting them carefully on the counter. It took two trips. There were seven weapons.

"I want to sell these," I said to the storeowner. "What can you give me?"

I knew the lot was worth at least a thousand dollars. The man checked them carefully, opening each chamber, peering down the barrel, keeping one eye on me at the same time.

"I'll give you a hundred bucks for them," he said. It was a ridiculously low offer.

"I'll gladly take it," I answered. My words shocked both of us. He wondered why I was content to take such a measly sum, and I wondered why I was so happy to give up what had been my only real security in life. I had loved the guns, always carrying at least one with me since my return from Vietnam.

The gun shop owner handed me five twenty-dollar bills. I walked out, whistling, feeling even more free. Another weight seemed to have fallen from my shoulders.

I strolled down the street and passed a barbershop. Examining myself in the window, I decided my hair needed a trim. A chair was open, so I walked in and climbed up. The barber tightened the cloth around my neck and began to clip away.

"Beautiful day, isn't it?" I said. I felt so good I wanted to hug everybody I saw. I chirped away until he finished, even telling him about some of the events of the previous day. He just went on clipping; I think he had heard every possible story at least once and wasn't too interested in mine.

It was now mid-afternoon, and I decided to travel back to Oakleigh for the evening. I passed by Waynesboro again and arrived at the mansion at 5:30. About a dozen people lived full-time at the house, and when I walked in they were eating supper.

"Hey! Look who's here," one of them called out. "Come in and eat with us, Glenn. Good to see you!"

I sat down and joined the table conversation. A girl named Lenea came with a place setting, and food was passed. When the meal ended several of us continued to talk. I explained again how, as long as I could remember, I had been enslaved by fear. I asked them if I would ever feel that way again, now that I was a Christian.

"The Lord will protect you against those things if you ask him," Lenea said. "He gives us a helper, the Holy Spirit."

"That sounds good," I said.

"Would you like us to pray with you that God will give you the strength—through the Holy Spirit—not to be afraid or worry anymore?" Lenea went on.

"Sure, why not?" I answered.

Several of them gathered around, placing their hands on my head and shoulders. Someone began to pray, and as I listened to the words, I lapsed for some moments into what appeared to be a dream.

In this dream I was in a body of water, far from shore. I bobbed up and down, unable to move. I began to sink and struggle. Fear gripped me. I was drowning. This predicament was peculiar, because in reality I am a powerful swimmer. Now I was helpless. I began to scream "Help! Help me!" and then a hand appeared and lifted me above the water's surface. I began to move, actually walking on the water, and I realized someone was next to me. A man, his hand wrapped around my waist, was holding me up. We began to talk, and as he spoke, it seemed as though love were being poured into me. Finally we reached the beach.

"Glenn, I will be with you always," he said. He disappeared, and my dream ended.

After the prayer, I told the others what I had seen and heard. They were amazed and happy.

"You must have just had a talk with Jesus," Lenea said.

I was shaken by the experience, not sure what had happened. All I knew was that strong and powerful—and good—events were taking place.

After the evening's Bible study, we prayed some more. "Could you pray that I'll get a job?" I asked. My trial for using the mail to threaten Brandon White was only nine days away, and I knew I certainly would be sent to prison if I had to face the judge without employment. We prayed, and then I said good night to the brothers and sisters.

I drove home to Aunt Sarah's house in Waynesboro. She was relieved to see me. I had been away for more than a week. Aunt Sarah thought I might be dead, finally wiped out in an alley brawl or a flaming car wreck. She looked me over carefully, very pleased that for once I had come home clean and in good spirits.

Tuesday morning my former boss at the fast-food restaurant called.

"Glenn, could you come into work tomorrow?" he asked.

"Sure. You still want me to be assistant manager?"

"No. You lost your chance at that job. I need a janitor."

I remembered how we had prayed about my job the night before at Oakleigh, so I figured this must be the answer.

"OK, I'll come in. Bye."

One of my new friends at Oakleigh had told me on Sunday that all my problems wouldn't disappear just because I was a Christian. "You'll probably even have some new ones," he had said. I believed him now. Going back to the restaurant would be tough. When I was a manager I had been mean to my workers, cursing them and forcing them to do dirty, unnecessary cleanup jobs if I didn't like them or thought they were slacking. Now I would be on their level, working with them side-by-side. I didn't look forward to it; but I did have a job, and I thanked God for it.

That afternoon I drove out in the country to visit Henry and Virginia Wingfield. Over the years, I had stayed in contact with them, stopping now and then to talk. When Henry saw my beaming face he knew something was up.

"You look different," Henry said as I walked toward him.

"You're my brother now, Henry," I said. "I've accepted Christ into my heart."

Henry laughed heartily, clamped my hand vigorously, and slapped me on the back. "That's just great, Glenn. Wayne Lawton will want to know about this."

That night I called Wayne, who had moved to Maryland.

"Praise God!" he said. "I've been praying for you for years."

Wayne asked me to look up the new Free Methodist minister in Waynesboro, David Stout. "Be sure to spend time with mature Christians, Glenn," Wayne said. "Dave will help you."

The next morning at seven I reported for work at the restaurant. The teen-agers working there laughed when they saw me haul the garbage cans outside. My pride was hurt, and for a moment I wanted to punch somebody's face or just walk off the job. But I needed work, and I didn't need more trouble. So I vented my humiliation by scrubbing the cans vigorously. I began to think about the recent changes in my life, and before long was humming and singing a song I'd learned at Oakleigh.

> Oh how I love Jesus,
> Oh how I love Jesus,
> Oh how I love Jesus,
> Because he first loved me.

One of my coworkers, a flippant high school boy I had picked on in the past, heard me singing.

"Man, what have you been smoking?" he asked, his mouth gaping open in disbelief. "You've flipped out!"

"Nothin's the matter," I answered. "I'm just happy. I love everybody. I love you, because I know God loves me."

The kid shook his head. "The guy has cracked," he muttered to himself as he hurried back into the building. I laughed.

Each evening I commuted back and forth to Oakleigh. Many nights I ate supper with my friends there, and sometimes when a discussion would run late, I would stay overnight in a spare room in the mansion.

My interest in the Bible was intense. I had read the Bible when I was a child but never understood it. Now, with help from my new friends, the book was making some sense. I learned that God would not punish me for mistakes my parents had made but wanted to change me so I would not repeat the same errors. Some Scriptures I especially enjoyed, like "I will never leave you nor forsake you." A teacher at Oakleigh told me Jesus had said this. I never wanted him to leave me.

On July 8, two days before my trial was to begin, I asked

those at Oakleigh to pray that if I had to go to jail, at least Jesus would go with me. Ten of us gathered together; several prayed that God's will concerning the trial would be done.

I met again with my lawyer. When first charged with the felony, I had asked him to argue every legal technicality in trying to get me freed. But after meeting Jesus Christ, I decided to plead guilty and accept my punishment.

"You're taking a real chance," the lawyer said, "but I'll do what I can."

On July 10 I appeared in court and pled guilty. The judge had every page of my record spread before him. He had studied it all—the mental hospitals, the juvenile charges, the army, everything. Now I was a new person in Christ, but my past could not be changed. My history was pathetic. I expected the judge to think me hopeless and dangerous, a menace to society.

The judge questioned me several minutes, then asked my lawyer and me to come and stand before the bench. The judge, a middle-aged man with a pale, deadpan face, peered down at me for a moment. No one moved. Quiet ruled the room. Finally he spoke.

"Glenn Hester, first of all I find you guilty as charged and sentence you to five years in the federal penitentiary."

I quivered inside but held myself in check. *Thank you, Lord,* I thought. *I know you will go with me.* I was scared, though. I hated to leave my new friends at Oakleigh.

"Second," the judge continued, "and I don't really know why I'm doing this, I'm going to suspend the sentence."

I could not believe what I was hearing.

"I'm putting you on three years' probation and placing you under the Young Men's Offenders Act. If you can make it through the next three years without problems with the law and fulfill the obligations of probation—and I doubt you will, Mr. Hester—the court will drop all charges."

I wanted to cry tears of joy. The judge also told me I must see a psychologist twice a week during the probation period. "If you miss one appointment with the psychologist, if you get one speeding ticket, if you get even a parking ticket—you're going to jail. Do you understand me, young man?" the judge concluded.

"Yes, Your Honor," I replied, wanting to dance a jig and kiss somebody, especially the judge. My lawyer shook my hand, and I left the courtroom a free man.

When I went to Oakleigh that night and told about the trial, the others broke into applause and several said, "Praise the Lord!"

A week later on my day off, in the afternoon I drove out from Waynesboro to see the Heatwoles. I had not visited with them since Mary Ann's funeral, and I knew they would be happy to hear of my new life.

"Yup, Mr. Heatwole, I'm really born again now!" I said as we sat in the parlor, the same room where Mary Ann and I had talked six years before.

"I'm so pleased for you, Glenn," he said. "We've prayed many times that you would find the Lord." When I left, Mrs. Heatwole gave me a hug. I saw tears sparkling in her eyes. There were some in mine, too.

My visits began with the psychologist, a short, curly-haired young doctor from New York City named David Silverman. I liked Dr. Silverman and appreciated his counseling. But many times his advice seemed to clash with my emerging Christian faith. I had become acquainted with the Free Methodist minister Dave Stout and his wife, Mary, and often discussed the psychologist's ideas with them. Dave and Mary always tried to weigh any idea against what the Bible said.

One evening, after one of the many meals Mary fed me, Dave and I were sitting at the kitchen table talking. For some time I had been recalling and was bothered by all the dirty tricks I had pulled over the years—beating up people, stealing money, chasing married women, selling liquor illegally. I knew God had forgiven me, but I still felt guilty and wanted to make things right. I asked Dave what I should do.

"God wants you to make up as many of those things as you can, Glenn," Dave said.

His words sobered me. In my wild days I had made many enemies, and if I admitted a crime to any of them and the police were notified, I would be on my way to prison.

I asked Silverman, too, what I should do.

"If you've got a guilty conscience, go put some money in the poor box or give it to charity. That should help you feel better," he said.

Dave Stout didn't agree. "What is going to be the basis for how you live? The psychologist's words or God's?" he asked.

I knew the answer. I started contacting people I owed something to. There were many names on my list.

The first one was Mother, who still lived in New York. I wrote her a three-page letter telling how I had hated her for years but now was commanded by Christ to forgive others for past wrongs. I told her I still felt hurt about the way she had treated me when I was a child, but I wanted— with God's help—to put that agony behind me. I told Mother I loved her.

Next I went looking for Earl Taylor, owner of the cab company I had driven for. I had shortchanged the company consistently by not turning in the correct fare money. One evening in September I rang the bell at Earl's home. His wife opened the door.

"Mrs. Taylor, is your husband home?" I asked. She went back inside to find him, leaving me standing on the step. He came, finally.

"Hi, Earl."

"What do you want, Hester?" Earl said, his face tensing. He and I had squabbled constantly, and I had quit driving cabs for him only because I knew he planned to fire me.

"Earl, here's seventy-five dollars. I think this is about how much I stole from you."

"What?" Earl said, rubbing his chin as he peered out the screen door.

"I'm a Christian now, and I know I should pay you back. If you want to call the police and have them come and arrest me for stealing, I'll be glad to wait here."

"Nah, forget it." He cracked the door, reached his hand out and took the bills, then walked away.

Mrs. Taylor had remained standing near the door. In a tender voice she said, "I hope the Lord blesses you for what you just did."

Paying money back to people raised my spirits, but my bank account sank to near zero. I was paying child support for my two children in addition to caring for my own needs. The pay for janitorial work at the restaurant was meager. I finally quit and found a better paying job at a warehouse.

My outlook on life was new, but I still had many old bad habits. Worst was my explosive temper, which often bested me. I still wanted to rely on my fists rather than God's power to solve problems. One day at the warehouse, while moving some heavy crates, I was singing about Jesus. My voice has a nasal quality, and Jody, one of my workmates, didn't appreciate my vocal artistry or the song's message.

"Reverend Goody-Goody," Jody said to me, "would you turn down the volume on the church music. This isn't Sunday."

His words angered me. I didn't want anybody to make fun of Jesus—or me.

"Hey, what's the matter, Bud? Does the song make you worry about going to hell?" I yelled back.

He rushed me and hit me in the face. I fell backwards and was about to take after him when some other workers grabbed my arms and held me until I cooled. In the past I would have found a way to get revenge. Now, after my anger subsided, I felt bad, sick inside that I had acted so foolishly. I found Jody later and told him I was sorry.

That evening I saw Dave Stout. "What happened to your face?" he asked. By now my eye was blackened.

"I had another fight about God," I said. "But this time I didn't hit back!"

Dave laughed. He knew how hard I was struggling to change my ways. We often talked about how I needed to learn to turn the other cheek and forgive.

"Bitterness towards others is like an acid eating away your soul," Dave said once. "If you don't forgive people, it's as if you're a jailer who is keeping them in a dungeon. As long as those people are in their cells, you have to stay and guard them. But if you free them through forgiveness, you can close the jail, leave, and be free yourself."

Dave's advice made sense to me. I continued to look up people to whom I owed things. Many of them I didn't see very often since I no longer hung out in the bars. As with the desire to smoke, my taste for alcohol was gone.

Now and then I would meet one of my former lady friends on the street or in a store. I told them all I wouldn't be running and chasing anymore: "I belong to Jesus Christ now. He doesn't want me messin' around."

Most of these women probably thought I had to be looped out on drugs to be saying such strange things. In time, though, they learned I had meant what I said. They didn't see me anymore.

The most surprised people with whom I shared my new faith were several members of the Waynesboro Police Department. The officers just could not figure me out. Instead of chasing me away from bar fights, they now saw me strolling the streets with a Bible in hand, stopping to chat with little kids and older ladies.

Oakleigh remained my second home. I had been baptized in a pond there and attended services in the mansion nearly every week. But in September I began to believe strongly that God wanted me to join Dave Stout's Free Methodist Church. I had good friends there, like the Wingfields, and I loved Dave and Mary. The sisters and brothers at Oakleigh thought this was a good idea, too, and encouraged me to take the step. So I did. Only three months had passed since the end of my wild-living days, but there I was, warming a pew every time the church door opened!

I visited a number of other churches in the area, too.

Many times, after I introduced myself and talked with the pastor, I was asked to tell my story to the congregation. I especially enjoyed speaking to young people. I warned them not to go down the destructive paths I had walked, but to get close to God.

Sometimes after these services, people would come up to tell me I spoke so enthusiastically I should consider becoming a minister. I appreciated the sentiment but laughed at these comments. I had a poor education, no money, and was on probation for a felony. These didn't seem to be good qualifications for the ministry.

But I couldn't suppress my desire to learn more about God and the Bible. I began to pray and dream about attending Bible school or college. I had too little faith to believe such a wild prayer would be answered.

God evidently thought otherwise.

14. Give Him All You've Got!

Charlottesville, Virginia, March, 1974

The trees at Oakleigh groaned under a heavy, late winter snowfall. I parked my car and picked my way through the snow. In the distance the sound of singing flowed vibrantly from the mansion. It was Sunday, and several weeks had passed since I last visited with my friends.

During the morning worship service, in a time set aside for sharing, I told of my recent experiences and of what Jesus had been teaching me. I said nothing about my future. I wanted so badly to ask for prayer about my desire to attend college, but I was self-conscious, hesitant to mention what to me was an absurd idea.

After the service, a couple, Donald and Linda Shanhaltzer, came up to me. "Glenn, we believe the Lord wants you to attend college," Don said. "And we're so convinced of it, we want to help pay your way!"

I wanted to laugh and cry all at once. His words encouraged me, but nothing could change the fact I was, at best, highly questionable college material. My formal education had ended after tenth grade. Only recently I had barely passed a GED test to get a high school diploma. Besides that, I had little money.

But in my heart I wanted to go to school, so I wrote to two Christian colleges. In a diplomatic way, both turned me down. Neither believed I could handle college work.

One Sunday I visited another church in Waynesboro. As I spoke with the pastor after the service, I was surprised when he too asked if I had any interest in a college education.

"Yes, I do," I answered, "but colleges aren't interested in me."

"I know of a college—Lee College in Tennessee—that might want you," he said.

I wrote to the admissions office of the school and received a moderately encouraging reply. The school suggested I come for a personal interview.

An April date was set. My probation officer gave permission for the trip, and a friend from Oakleigh, Kirt Kirtland, took time off from his job to help me drive the five-hundred-mile trip to Cleveland, Tennessee.

When I told my interviewers at Lee about my past lifestyle, my poor study habits, and lack of self-discipline, I could tell they were apprehensive. If accepted at Lee, I would be a twenty-six-year-old freshman with a history of mental illness and low scholastic aptitude. They needed time to discuss my case; I was excused to visit the campus and asked to return after lunch.

When I entered the office again, the two interviewers smiled.

"Glenn, we've decided to admit you as a full-time student," the admissions director said. "But there are some things we must insist you do."

I nodded my head eagerly.

"First, we'll need a written release from your psychologist. He needs to tell us if you can stand up under the pressures of school. Then, when you come here, we want you to receive extensive academic and personal counseling. We want Lee to be a positive experience for you."

I must have floated from the room. "Can you believe this?" I said to Kirt as we drove the long haul back to Virginia. "Glenn no-good-bum Hester is going to be a student at a *Christian* college!"

Back in Waynesboro, I headed for Dr. Silverman's office. I could tell he thought my becoming "Joe College" was humorous, but he had always suggested more education for me and so was pleased. He asked some questions about the school and then wrote the required letter. Some months later my counselor at Lee told me Silverman had written: "I don't personally believe in this 'Jesus stuff.' But if this 'Jesus stuff' will keep Glenn Hester straight, give him all you've got!"

My next visit was with my probation officer. He was skeptical and wondered, I suppose, what kind of scheme I had hatched to leave Virginia and escape his supervision. I convinced him finally by proving I could support myself financially on a small work scholarship from the college and my GI bill.

The people at the Free Methodist church and Oakleigh were overjoyed. Joann Carroll, a woman in the Waynes-boro church who was like a mother to me, became so excited she bought me some new clothes and even offered to help pay my way.

The remainder of the summer I continued to visit small churches in the area, sharing my story at every opportunity. Normally I ended my talk by mentioning I was about to start college—maybe to become a minister. Afterward, people often approached me saying they wanted to help support me financially. I was amazed at how God was showering love on me through his people.

In August, three weeks before leaving for my freshman year, I visited Oakleigh for an evening Bible study. I arrived full of joy, overflowing with gratitude to God for meeting my needs and giving me a chance to go to school. A girl named Heath was at the meeting. Before we all prayed together, she asked God to provide her some type of transportation so she could get back and forth to work. I knew instantly how God would answer her prayer.

After the meeting I found Heath. "How would you like to have a car?" I asked her. "It's only a 1968 Ford, and it's not the best looking thing in the world, but it runs."

Heath didn't know what to say. Finally, she said: "You can't mean it?"

"I do. Here are the keys. I hope you enjoy it."

The happiness glowing on her face filled me even further

with joy. I would have given her a new Cadillac if that had been possible. More and more I longed to pass on the love my father in heaven was giving to me, to help others as I had been helped.

In September I packed my two suitcases and several boxes and rode to Tennessee with three other freshmen from Waynesboro. Being eight years older than the others, I almost felt like their father. But before long I joined in on the teasing and joking as we rode along.

At Lee I settled in, sharing a dormitory room with one of the students from Waynesboro. I signed up for classes, bought my books, and met my counselor, David Black. David suggested we meet each week for several hours just to talk. I liked his easygoing, friendly manner.

Twelve hundred students attended Lee, and before long I knew many of them. From the first I felt part of a family— a family that included not only students but staff members, too. One of the music professors, Bertha Gugler, showed great courage (being I can't carry a tune) and invited me to sing in the choir at the Methodist church we both attended. We became friends, and she and her husband invited me to their home many times. Everywhere on campus people greeted me by name and showed interest in my unusual needs. I felt accepted.

The college was operated by the Church of God, but many faculty and staff members were from other denominational backgrounds. I enrolled in Bible, Christian education, theology, and ministerial classes, as well as in general subjects like American history—my favorite. Always eager to express myself, I thrived on classroom discussions.

Chapel services were held three times a week, and day after day I was exposed to more of the Word of God.

One sparkling October day, when the fall air was crisp and the leaves flaming orange, red, and yellow, I was returning to the dormitory at noon. I passed a woman futilely trying to start her car.

"Hi, can I help you?" I asked. I recognized the lady. It was Mrs. Gertrude Aldrich, the dean of women.

"Oh, please!" she answered.

I opened the hood and listened. I heard metal scraping against metal and a clicking noise.

"It's the starter, Mrs. Aldrich. It's shot. You'll need to replace it. If you want me to, I'll fix it."

"That would be wonderful, Glenn, if it's not too much trouble."

After my last class that afternoon, I obtained the parts and made the repair. I rode with Mrs. Aldrich back to her home and she served a snack. We talked as we ate, and I told her about my past. Before I left she wanted to pay me, but I refused. Just being a guest in her home and being listened to was worth much more.

"Any time you need a car, Glenn," she said as I walked out the door, "you can use mine."

On my way back to campus, I had to smile. I had given away my old car, and now the Lord had arranged for me to use a newer model. I did borrow it, too—many times!

College life agreed with me: the rolling, neatly clipped lawns spotted with trees; the pretty girls and new friends; the stately buildings decorated with ivy; the bull sessions at the dorm; the convocations; and the counseling with Mr. Black. My classes interested me, too, and I was steadily learning. But even with heavy tutoring, I was struggling to pass. I did not know how to study and used any excuse to leave my books unopened. When a discussion started in somebody's room at the dorm, chances were good I would be there before long. I could talk and listen for hours, and my grades showed it.

In counseling with Mr. Black, I was peeling away the coverings on past memories, each layer bringing to light a new group of persons who had hurt me and whom I needed to forgive. I had Jesus Christ in my life, but I still had those memories. Most of them centered on hate and revenge. I struggled to forgive, calling to mind one person after another, and praying for strength to bury each sadness.

"You've got to trust God, forgive, and take authority over

your problems," Mr. Black said repeatedly. "Do circumstances control you, or is it the opposite?"

Slowly that first semester, I learned to do what he suggested. But the strain of recalling my past together with the pressures of school caused me to have stomach pains severe enough for a week's hospitalization. During visiting hours my room was full as students and teachers stopped in to wish me well and keep me up to date on what was happening on campus.

The semester ended; and after struggling through final exams, I was left with an unimpressive collection of C's and D's on my grade sheet. But I loved the school and looked forward to the spring term.

Second semester registration day came. I didn't have enough money to pay tuition, and my GI bill check wasn't due for several weeks. I was stumped. I visited a local bank, hoping to arrange a short-term loan, but the loan officer refused because I was jobless and had no credit references.

The next day while hiking by a campus fountain, I met one of my teachers, Bill Snell. We chatted for a moment, and I mentioned I was short on funds.

"I can help you with that," he said without hesitation. "Go downtown to First Security Bank and see Mark Hamilton. Tell him you want a loan, and that Bill Snell will sign it."

Professor Snell walked off. I was taken aback, and unusual for me, had thought of nothing to say—not even thank you. He hadn't even asked how much I wanted to borrow.

I hurried to the bank and saw Mr. Hamilton. After saying the magic words "Bill Snell" the response was quick.

"How much do you need, Mr. Hester?" the loan officer asked.

"Three hundred dollars."

"Do you want that in cash or check?"

"Check, please," I said, my voice squeaking.

The pay-back arrangements were completed. As I stood to leave, Mr. Hamilton said casually: "Oh, when you have a chance, have Bill sign this note and bring it in."

I grasped the paper and walked out dazed. Later I gave the loan note to Professor Snell. He never again said one word to me about the money or asked whether I had paid it back or not—which I did. I was awed that he could trust someone like me so very much.

My friends in Virginia did not forget me either. Week after week my basic needs were met as individuals and families sent small gifts of money, many of them coming as a surprise. The letters cheered me the most, though, with their kindly worded messages of love. Less than two years before when I was roaming the streets of Waynesboro, I might have cursed or even knifed anyone who dared to say she or he loved me. In those days I had thought such talk showed weakness. Now I understood what it really was, a sign of unequalled strength, the power of God's love.

I wanted to stay at Lee, but in the second semester I sensed again an urge to move along. Could Jesus have some other place for me to go? I had come to Lee thinking I should study to be a minister. One afternoon in homiletics class, the professor helped me clarify just what type of minister I was to be.

"Listen carefully to this, my friends," he said, leaning forward over his podium and holding each of us with his eyes. "If you think you might like doing anything else besides being a minister, then do that. Being a minister is a full-time job. You won't have time for other activities. You'll be frustrated and ineffective. You must know you've been called."

His words penetrated my thoughts and made me question my motives. I knew Jesus wanted me to be his witness; but I was certain, even though I loved to talk and preach at people, that I had never been called to be a minister. What I really wanted to do was learn a trade and work with my hands. I had not forgotten those happy days at the plumbing shop, working beside Tom.

But where should I go? Not long after the illuminating day in homiletics class, I stopped by the jobs board in front of the college's placement office. One notice caught my eye:

WANTED: Dedicated Christian workers for rewarding ministry with youth in New York City. Contact David Wilkerson, Teen Challenge, 444 Clinton Avenue, Brooklyn, N.Y.

I dreaded even considering a return to New York City, but I wrote and inquired, explaining my qualifications in auto mechanics and other equipment repair. A letter came back promptly. Teen Challenge needed someone to care for vehicles and buildings. Would I be interested?

My friends and I at Lee prayed about my future. It became clear God wanted me back in New York. I sensed my turn had come to give out the love he had been filling me with in a Christian environment.

The school year ended. I stayed on for a few weeks, taking several short courses. As it came time to leave, I sadly packed my bags. Then I thanked and said good-bye one by one to the many members of my loving family at Lee.

My short college career was over. But what I had learned through watching my Christian brothers and sisters in action would last me a lifetime.

15. A Special Gift

New York City, August, 1975

The sight of the New York skyline, looming miles ahead, should have excited me—after all, the city was my home. But as the Trailways bus rumbled across the bridge from New Jersey that August afternoon, I was anxious, troubled by a deep stirring of unease about how the city's evils might claw away at my new Christian life.

Having crossed the Hudson River, the bus slowed in heavier traffic. Already I was homesick for Lee College and Virginia. On my trip north from Tennessee, I had stopped in Waynesboro for two weeks. I visited and played with my kids again. I attended the Free Methodist church and Oakleigh and spent hours catching up on news with my friends. Since I would be a volunteer with Teen Challenge and receive only a small salary, many people offered to continue sending me money for living expenses. Then I said good-bye to my children, giving them a last, long hug. I boarded a northbound bus at the Waynesboro depot, site of so many of my sad departures.

In Manhattan my bus crept along the jammed streets, nearing the Port Authority terminal. Gazing out the window at the thousands of people rushing along sidewalks, I recalled how while growing up I had run so many times from my problems, catching buses going anywhere just to get away. Now I was on a bus coming *in,* feeling some fear, but coming as a free man with a purpose. And this time I was not alone; Jesus was with me.

The bus docked. A volunteer worker from Teen Challenge met me. I claimed my bags, and we drove to Brooklyn, headquarters for the organization in New York. Teen

Challenge was housed in several buildings in a predominantly black neighborhood.

Although I had grown up in New York I had never heard of Teen Challenge until, after becoming a Christian, I had read the book *The Cross and the Switchblade* by David Wilkerson. I believed I could communicate effectively with the street kids Teen Challenge worked with. I, too, once had known their hatreds and hopelessness.

My new boss, George Kelley, welcomed me to Teen Challenge and showed me where I would live, a small apartment in one of the buildings. George was the maintenance supervisor, a quiet, kind, salt-and-pepper-haired man in his mid-fifties. I was to be his assistant.

After dropping my bags in the apartment, George showed me through the buildings and introduced me to other staff members and kids as we went. He explained how I would be combining maintenance work with counseling of ex-drug addicts. When possible I would involve boys with me in repair duties. This would give me a chance to be a friend while helping them learn skills and how to work.

My first Saturday back in New York I hunted up a telephone directory and looked for Free Methodist churches. I was surprised to see only two listed—one of them obviously Spanish-speaking, the second an English-speaking congregation in Brooklyn. I wrote down the pastor's number at the Brooklyn church and called. A woman answered.

"Hello, Brooklyn Free Methodist."

"My name is Glenn Hester. I've just come to the city, and I was a member of a Free Methodist church in Virginia. I would like to visit your church. When are you havin' services tomorrow?"

"I'm just baby-sitting here for the pastor and his wife. I'm a member, though, too. Our Sunday morning service is at ten," she answered.

"I'll plan to come over tomorrow. I'm workin' at Teen Challenge. What's your name, by the way?"

"Carla . . . Carla Brauen."

"Well, nice talkin' to you, Carla. I'll see you tomorrow."

The next morning I walked to the church, arriving early at the crumbling, red concrete building wedged between houses on a residential street. A small group of people was in the sanctuary, at most twenty adults plus several children. Later I learned the church had nearly closed a few years earlier. Many former members had moved from the neighborhood. The service had not begun, and I was glad to see some younger people, several of them pretty girls, standing in a cluster, visiting.

I aggressively introduced myself, hugging everyone within reach and planting a "brotherly" kiss on the cheek of each girl. The "kiss of peace" had always been a part of greetings at Oakleigh, but as I gently smacked each girl I could tell by their reaction that the custom was foreign here. One of the girls, the one named Carla whom I had spoken with on the phone, even seemed perturbed about it.

I joined in eagerly with the singing and sharing. I left lighthearted, thinking that maybe I could survive as a Christian in New York after all.

My official duties at Teen Challenge began the next day. I helped maintain all of the heating and cooling equipment, repaired cars and trucks, did some electrical wiring, and watched over construction and maintenance projects done by outside contractors. I also was delegated to make certain the buildings and equipment were secure at all times. Theft and vandalism were continuing threats in our neighborhood.

I talked and counseled with the teen-agers whenever I could. At first they were skeptical; I didn't blame them. Some of them were from families who had lived on welfare for three generations. Day after day they spent seeking one high after another to escape the desolate reality of their life. I tried to help them learn how to work, how to get along with a boss, how to keep a job.

My efforts with the street kids often drained the small reservoir of patience the Holy Spirit had constructed in me. I, too, was still on the mend from a bombed-out childhood, was still being restored from some of the same catastrophes the kids were experiencing.

During my first week at Teen Challenge, I was trying one day to explain the benefits of hard work to three boys. The kids knew little about my past. One of them, an outgoing, talkative black named Martin, thought he had me pegged.

"Ah, man, you're just a typical white dude who never had no problems. Now you're steppin' in here in New York City to tell us how to solve our problems. Why don't you just leave us alone and go back where you came from?"

"Martin, you ever heard of Spofford?" I asked him. His eyes widened. He and the others knew a whole lot about Spofford. Many of them had spent time there. "I've been in there. I know this town, I know what's happenin' on the street. This place is tough, but with Christ you can survive—be somebody."

We sat down for a while, tapping the tools we had been working with on the floor as we talked. I told them some of my story. When I finished, the boys were quiet. Seeing a glimmer of respect in their faces, I understood better why God had brought me back to the city.

One evening I decided to call Mother, who was now living alone in a small community about twenty miles north of the city. She was surprised to learn I had returned to New York. We talked a few minutes and set a date when I could come for a visit.

I drove to see her on a Saturday. We greeted each other awkwardly, exchanging a brief kiss and hug. We caught up on news of the family, and I explained my work with the boys at Teen Challenge. I told her the story of how I had become a follower of Jesus Christ and now lived for love rather than revenge.

Mother smiled at me, although I saw in her eyes some puzzlement, as though what I was saying was unclear to her.

"Mother, I'm sorry for all the things I did to you," I said, "and I won't blame you anymore for what happened when I was little."

Mother didn't speak, just went on smiling.

The time to leave came. I stood by the door of her apartment, wanting to say one more thing.

"Mother . . . I love you."

She walked to me and we embraced. "I love you, too, Glenn, and I'm so proud of you."

I left, thankful that with the love of God even the gaping chasm separating me from my mother might someday be bridged.

Each Sunday I attended the Brooklyn Free Methodist Church. By the end of each week I needed some time away from the pressures at Teen Challenge, and I enjoyed the intimacy of the small congregation. I was forming friendships there, and one girl in particular was playing a major role in my thoughts—Carla, the same one I had first talked to on the phone.

I liked Carla. She had long, red hair, which she sometimes tied in braids. She was quiet and shy, gentle and delicate in manner. Carla had grown up in Yorkshire, a small town in upstate New York. After completing college with a major in social work four years before, she had come to the city to find work. I tried clumsily to make a positive impression on her—and failed. It seemed I was not the man of her dreams.

One Sunday after the church service I was talking to Carla, hinting to her that I would like to do some sightseeing in New York, such as visit the Statue of Liberty. Since I had just moved up from Virginia, she wasn't yet aware I had lived for nearly sixteen years in the New York area. Probably feeling sorry for me, she finally agreed to give me a short tour of Manhattan. We picked a date, a Saturday near the end of September.

I think Carla dreaded our upcoming rendezvous, but I was eager and confident. My being a Christian had not changed one thing: I was a normal young man who welcomed the company of a pretty young woman. And, I must admit, I still thought of myself as being quite gifted in the ways of romance.

The big day arrived. Carla and I met, then boarded the subway. We chatted as we rode, and it seemed we were having a great time. I tried to be funny and clever, and sometimes she laughed. We left the subway and walked to the ferry dock. By this time I thought Carla was thrilled to be with me and our relationship had flowered.

The sky was clear, the afternoon breeze warm. The ferry's horn sounded, and as we glided toward the statue, gulls soared and dipped in the boat's wake. My spirits were soaring, too; I turned to Carla, smiled widely, and gently, oh so smoothly, tried to hold her hand.

"Oh, I'd rather not," she said with a pained look, pulling her hand away.

I was surprised, momentarily made speechless by the rebuff. But I recovered fast. I liked her too much to give up easily. I resumed my jokes but didn't try to hold her hand again that day.

My work at Teen Challenge continued to be rewarding but not without strains. I still struggled with my short-fuse temper. The street kids learned how to provoke me, using bad language and talking back. At times I blew up, grabbing a kid by the neck or arm and forcing him to do what I wanted. Twice I actually traded punches with one of them—a situation I painfully regretted later. Although my pride rebelled, I always went back and said I was sorry, trying to explain how my old, rotten nature had gotten the best of me.

Mr. Kelley, who became like a father to me, helped me see how wrong it was to resort to violence. To do so was to play the game with the same rules the teen-agers lived by. As a Christian I had something different to offer.

"When you raise your fists, Glenn, you're just defending your old self. That part of you has to die," Mr. Kelley told me more than once.

He was right. I prayed for more patience. Slowly I learned to control myself better and ignore calculated taunts. Jesus helped me to love the teen-agers I counseled, to serve them—even when I felt like knocking their teeth out.

On weekends I worked with my friends at the church. Several new young people joined, and all of us began to visit with and try to help people in the neighborhood. Hundreds of children lived within walking distance of the church building, and we began recruiting them for Sunday school.

My mind was still on Carla. I was in love with her, and my feelings were no secret among members of the small church. Carla remained cool, apparently not interested in her rowdy suitor, although I thought the ice was thawing slightly.

By the end of October, even though Carla seldom found time to date me, I began to think seriously about marrying her. I visited a religious bookstore, bought four books on Christian marriage, and started my homework. At last I had found a subject that held my attention, one I didn't mind studying for hours.

Thankfully, my friends at the church began to tell Carla of my good qualities, encouraging her to keep an open mind.

After attending a seminar on youth problems and the family, I asked several other members of the church—including Carla—if we could meet on Saturday nights to study these topics and have prayer. These meetings started and, to my delight, Carla often invited me to join her and another friend for supper before the weekly discussions.

I had become involved with CURE (Christian Urban Renewal Effort), an offshoot of Teen Challenge. CURE operated a ministry center on 105th Street in Spanish Harlem. This was a tough place to bring Christ's love, but progress was being made. Young prostitutes and drug addicts were coming off the street for food, counseling, and spiritual help.

But the pimps and pushers in the area didn't think such efforts represented progress. One night in October, a local gang smashed all of the center's windows and set the building on fire. The heavy damage forced the center to close. The police did nothing. In high crime areas like this one, they didn't even bother to investigate "petty" crimes. They only had time for murders. It was too dangerous for them to hang around the area writing parking tickets and chasing burglars.

Two other workers and myself went to the partially burned-out building to clean up. Broken glass covered the floors, and the furniture was charred. Water had soaked everything when the firemen doused the blaze. We started shoveling, sweeping, and mopping. A young boy walked by on the sidewalk and yelled inside to me, "Hey! Come out here. You wanna see who started the fire?" I dropped my broom and hurried outside.

"See that little dude down there?" he pointed at a short, wiry teen-aged boy standing on the sidewalk with six others. "His name is Shorty. He did it."

My anger bubbled. I prayed for patience and not to lose my cool. I walked quickly toward the gang.

"Hey, your name Shorty?" I said, confronting him.

"Yeah, what about it?" he answered, his expression hard and cold.

"I understand you started the fire?"

"I don't know nothin' about no fire."

"Hey, Buddy, I know you did it. Why'd you do it?" I raised my voice, stepping toward him. "You ain't just messin' with people by startin' that fire. You're messin' with God."

"Bug off, Mister."

"No, I'm not done yet. Don't mess with God, man. He's got power, and the people you're botherin' in this building are his people."

He thought a moment. "OK, I lit up the buildin'. Look, I was paid by the pimps to do it. They don't like losin' their girls to the place. But I don't want God mad—no way. I'll help you clean up."

He came back with me and brought his friends. As we

worked together, Shorty told me some things about himself. He had no family and his home was the streets. He hustled money any way he could to get by. I told him of Jesus, how his life could be changed, how he could have hope. Shorty listened, but he just could not believe it.

The center reopened, and now and then Shorty would drop in. Darkness was settling on his life. I knew it would be just a matter of time before some tragedy swallowed him. I asked Shorty to come live in my apartment for a while. I knew if I pulled him off the street, maybe got him back in school, he might have a chance. But he wouldn't do it. As bad as it was, the street was all he knew, it was his life. After some months Shorty didn't come by anymore.

In November, Carla and I began to date more frequently, and after Thanksgiving I tried my "hint routine" again, this time mentioning how I had nowhere to go for the Christmas holidays. I badly wanted to be with her, to visit her home, and to meet my potential inlaws.

Carla took pity on me and invited me to Yorkshire for Christmas. On December 20, her parents, Carl and Leah Jean Brauen, drove down to the city to take her home. I had to work several more days and planned to come later. I met the Brauens on Sunday morning at church, then we all went to Carla's apartment for lunch. Since she was their oldest daughter, I sensed it would take quite a man to convince Mom and Dad he was "the one" for her.

The table conversation started out awkwardly, but before long I loosened up and seemed to be charming them with anecdotes about New York City and stories from my work at Teen Challenge. Wanting especially to impress Carla's parents with the uniqueness of my intervention in their daughter's life, I talked at length about how God, before he had called me to New York, had in an unusual way placed me in the Free Methodist church. Then, God certainly had showed his hand by bringing me—in a city of seven million people—to a congregation with forty members.

I paused a second before I said, in a serious, almost pious

tone, "I believe God brought me to this church so I could meet *Alice*."

My speech was over. I leaned back, pleased with myself until I realized I had just referred to Carla using the name of my ex-wife. After some nervous coughs and chopped sentences explaining my goof, I lapsed into near silence and remained subdued the rest of the afternoon.

By the time the church's Christmas program was held that evening, however, I had regained my confidence. We sat together in the same row in the sanctuary, singing carols and enjoying the songs sung by the children. Afterwards I said good-bye to Carla and her parents. They drove to Yorkshire the next day.

On Christmas Eve day I caught a ride with some friends to Carla's home. On arrival my rapport with Mary, one of her sisters, was immediately warm. She was a foster child who had lived with the Brauens since age two. Several presents with my name on them were with a pile of others under the tree, and I felt welcome. By the time I left several days later, I knew I would be part of a loving family—if I could just convince their eldest daughter to marry me.

Back in New York after the holidays, I finally gathered the courage to face an issue from my past that had bothered me for months. In 1969, long before I met Jesus, I had flown on a Piedmont Airlines flight to Charlottesville. After the plane landed, I walked to the baggage counter to claim the single bag I had checked. No one was inspecting the claim receipts, so I hustled the suitcase out to my car and walked back to the Piedmont baggage desk. I lied, telling the agent the airline had lost the bag. I fabricated a list of what it contained and filed the claim. About a month later Piedmont paid me $550 for the "lost" suitcase, which was sitting in my room. At the time I thought this robbery was a great joke.

Now, seven years later, I knew I had to pay Piedmont back. I called their headquarters in North Carolina and spoke with a customer service representative named Jackson Greene. I explained what had happened and concluded,

"I'm a follower of Jesus Christ now. He wants me to repay you."

"Ah, Mr. Hester, we'll have to check on this," Mr. Greene said, obviously unsure about what to say next. "This is quite unusual. Could I have your phone number? I'll call you back."

A week later Mr. Greene called. "You were right, Mr. Hester. I've verified the claim. We paid you $550. But since that was seven years ago, I'm sorry to tell you that with interest you now owe us $750. If you don't begin repayment, I'm afraid we'll have to seek prosecution of your case."

Seven hundred and fifty dollars! At Teen Challenge I was earning $45 a week, and from that I had to pay $60 a month for child support. I prayed about what to do. Then— when I knew I couldn't postpone it any longer—I called Mr. Greene.

"Mr. Greene, would it be okay with you if I paid the money back by installments?" I asked. "I could send you every other paycheck—seventy-five dollars a month. Would that be all right?"

He was silent a moment, thinking. "Yes, I think that will be fine. Why don't you call back in ten days or so, and we'll finalize the arrangements."

I talked with Mr. Greene several more times before everything was set. During our last call, by the way he kept extending the conversation I could tell he had something on his mind. Finally, he blurted it out.

"Glenn, I—ah—want to tell you something. I'm kind of, well, interested in Christianity. Don't get me wrong, I'm not religious . . ." His voice trailed off. I waited for him to continue.

"Before you called the first time, I had decided to— —uh—ask . . . pray that God would show me a Christian who really lived all this stuff. Then you called in. What you did made a big impression on me; I've decided to become a Christian. I just wanted to tell you, to thank you."

We spoke several minutes longer, then said good-bye.

Tears stung my eyes; I was shaken, humbled that God would use me in such a way.

In February I finally convinced Carla her future should involve a name change to Mrs. Glenn Hester. Carla was as cautious as I was impulsive. She wanted a long engagement (I think five to ten years would have pleased her), but we finally agreed on an October, 1976, wedding date. Carla thought we should spend more months getting to know each other. I couldn't blame her. My past qualified me more for prisoner's denims than a bridegroom's tuxedo.

We did talk. I shared my heart, everything from my troubled past. The more Carla listened, the more I talked. By early April it seemed she had heard enough. We decided to marry in May.

At 1:00 P.M. on May 29, the ceremony began at the Teen Challenge chapel in Brooklyn. Before the processional, the soloist sang Andrae Crouch's "My Tribute." Some of the words had special meaning for me.

> How can I say thanks
> for the things You have done for me?
> Things so undeserved
> Yet You gave to prove Your love for me.*

The song spoke for my heart, which was overflowing with thanksgiving.

Carla came down the aisle, dressed in flowing white, carrying a bouquet of daisies. She had woven several flowers into her hair. When I saw her and the smile on her face, I smiled too. I also thought, *Thank You, Lord, for making this moment possible, for changing my life, for giving me a special gift like Carla.*

The ceremony was brief. A friend played the trumpet. Carla and I exchanged vows, shared communion, kissed.

---

*MY TRIBUTE by Andrae Crouch © Copyright 1971 by LEXICON MUSIC, INC. ASCAP. All rights reserved. International copyright secured. Used by special permission.

With a wide grin on my face, I whisked Mrs. Glenn Hester down the aisle.

At the reception I embraced Mrs. Winston, my foster mother of years before, who had come with her son and his family to the wedding. Mr. Winston had been dead for several years. We reminisced about old times for a few minutes. Mother Winston was very happy for us.

Carla and I honeymooned in Pennsylvania. I had selected an exotic "lovers' hideaway" known, by startling coincidence, for good fishing. The fish didn't bite, but I scarcely noticed.

16. I Hear a Baby Crying

Brooklyn, September, 1976

At last, at age twenty-eight, I had a home of my own.
And in my home lived someone who loved me on good days
and bad. Carla earned my complete trust; and I began to
unwind, peeling away the emotional callouses on my true
feelings long buried deep inside. Jesus had saved me and
given me hope. Christian friends had supported me and
helped me mature. Now God used Carla to rebuild me
tenderly.

Living in New York, seeing again the familiar streets
and buildings, I remembered with aching sadness the
crushing of my hope as a child. Now that I had a home, I
recalled more vividly the agony of being without one. I
thought of those days at the Winstons, when my little boy's
world had crumbled and I had lost the security only found
in my mommy and daddy's arms.

In our apartment at Teen Challenge, Carla listened hour
after hour as I emptied out my bitterness. Before we married, Carla had learned the facts of my past. Now she
learned the feelings. Some nights I would dream of being
beaten as a child and would awaken screaming. Carla
would grab me and hold me close until I calmed. We would
pray together, asking Jesus to walk through my mind and
cast out the fearful memories.

Sometimes when we talked words would fail. Then I
could only bury my head in Carla's lap and weep. She held
me, softly encouraging me to cleanse my heart.

I dealt with those troubled years as a foster child. Before
my marriage, like most former foster children, I had
wanted to completely forget my childhood. But now I began

to think again about the happiness that had been stolen from me when I was just a baby. Newspaper stories and television programs on foster care and child abuse caught my attention. In my work at Teen Challenge I saw each day in the lives of twisted, broken kids what happens when children are not loved and guided and must find their own way.

Even with its frustrations, I loved this work. I believed I was having a good influence on the teen-agers; but in early 1977, I recognized that urge, the signal that God was preparing me for something new.

Carla and I prayed, and others did too, about what might be in store for the Hesters. While repairing vehicles and equipment, I had increasingly come to realize how little I really knew about fixing things. I loved using my hands, tearing machines apart and rebuilding them, but my knowledge was woefully incomplete. I needed more schooling—not college this time, but technical training. I resigned from Teen Challenge and enrolled in an automotive repair school in June, 1977.

Carla and I rented an apartment on the third floor of an older but well-kept house on 41st Street in Brooklyn. Saying good-bye to our friends at Teen Challenge was sad, but I was eager to begin school. Veterans' educational benefits helped meet our expenses, and Carla kept her job as a secretary for a lighting research institute in Manhattan. We tightened our belts, and I did odd jobs when possible to help out. Now that I was not an urban missionary, my faithful friends in Virginia no longer needed to send money.

Near Christmas I completed the automotive course and became a certified mechanic. I found a job with National Car Rental, working with other mechanics in the shop at LaGuardia Airport. Two months later the company set me up with my own shop in Manhattan. I did light maintenance and tune-up work on the rental cars.

While on my way home from work one day early in 1978, I stopped at a corner stand to buy a newspaper. I was disappointed that the paper I normally read, the New York *Daily News,* was sold out. Glumly I bought a copy of the New York *Times* instead. Unknowingly, I had done something significant—a small act that would alter my life.

Standing in the subway car, grasping the ceiling strap with one hand and the *Times* with the other, I skimmed the paper quickly. Only after dinner that evening, looking for something to read, did I pick up the newspaper again. I paged through. This time my eye stopped on a headline: FOSTER PARENTS ARE FORCED TO GIVE UP BOY THEY RAISED FOR TWO YEARS. Next to the story was a photo of a man holding a cute, dark-eyed boy with black, curly hair. Intrigued, I began to read.

> It was like telling someone their two-year-old child was dead when he was playing right in front of their eyes. . . .

I remembered the afternoon twenty-five years before when I had found my foster mother Mrs. Winston crying and had sensed that my little world was crumbling. I read more:

> The social worker looked sadly at the foster parents and said, "I have bad news for you. Pete is going back to his mother. . . ."

My heart ached. This sounded all too familiar. The article went on to explain how the foster parents, Mary and Steven Donnelly, had been led to believe the child they had cared for since shortly after his birth was adoptable. The placement agency involved was the very same one that had held me in their care, moving me from home to home when I was a boy.

"Carla," I yelled, "look at this!" I ran and showed her the newspaper. "Twenty-five years have gone by, and the same garbage is goin' on in foster care. Hasn't anybody learned what happens to these kids when you pass them around like unwanted pets?"

I was already angry, but I became roaring mad when I read the rest of the story. The Donnellys were a middle-class couple living in Queens. In 1976 they had decided to adopt a child and approached the child care agency, learning to their disappointment no applications for adoption were being accepted. However, they were told that if they took a child under temporary foster care, the chances for eventual adoption were very good.

The Donnellys underwent the routine investigation by the agency, and not long thereafter, were asked to take a fourteen-day-old boy named Pete. The woman they dealt with at the agency reportedly had told them chances for adoption were 99 to 1 in favor because the child's mother had been charged with neglecting two of her older children also in foster care. The Donnellys knew adoption was not an absolute certainty, but after two years passed they had ceased to fear their baby could be taken away.

The story sickened me. Although I had sympathy for the foster parents, my heart bled for little Pete. I could almost hear him crying. I knew not long ago little Pete had been me. As long as he could remember, there had been only one mommy and daddy in his world. Now, for reasons he could not understand, they were gone. Was he blaming himself? Was he having trouble sleeping? Was he forgetting his toilet training? Was he desperate from fear? How long would it be until he slammed the door to his emotions and stopped trying to love? What mental hospitals or prisons might await him? Would he someday fall in love with guns and then use them to unleash his rage on some innocent victim?

I feared for little Pete. I could not stay silent. I knew God wanted me to do something. I picked up the phone directory and found the number for the Donnellys. I dialed and a woman answered—her voice so weak I could scarcely hear her. She sounded upset. It was Mrs. Donnelly.

"Hi, my name is Glenn Hester. I've just read your story in the paper. I'm a former foster child who was cared for by the same agency that has Pete for over eleven years. I'm wondering if I could help you and your husband in any way?"

Mrs. Donnelly seemed to perk up, and her voice strengthened as she related the events leading up to the jerking of Pete from their home.

"Why did they let Pete's mother take him back when she had already neglected her other children?" I asked.

"Glenn, there's a sick, unbelievable law here in New York. It says the family court cannot let charges of abuse or neglect on *other* children influence a decision on a child who has not been mistreated. Of course Pete hasn't been abused by his mother. He's never lived with her!"

This was 1978, not the 1950s. Had there been no progress in foster care? Mrs. Donnelly went on.

"I would be less angry if I really thought Pete's mother had changed and wanted to give him a good home. But since we've had him, I've never seen any indication that she loves him. The few times she's visited him, I've almost had to force her to hold him."

Mrs. Donnelly started to cry, overcome again by her painful memories. "I worry about him, Glenn. And what about my husband and me? Who's going to put us back together again? We gave so much of our hearts and souls to him."

We talked a few minutes longer. I learned the Donnellys were to be guests on a local television discussion show to explain their story. Mrs. Donnelly invited me to meet the two of them at the studio.

"You won't be able to go on the show, but we wouldn't mind some support. You're an ex-foster child. Someone might listen to you," she said.

I agreed to come and said good-bye.

The next Monday I put on my suit and went to the television station where I met the Donnellys. We had about twenty-five minutes before the program went on the air, so we visited. Several other foster parents were present for support too.

The show began. Those of us who were not on the program watched on a monitor in a lounge down the hall from the studio. The male host introduced Mr. and Mrs. Donnelly, another foster parent, a representative of the foster care agency (the director of child placement), and another foster mother speaking on behalf of the agency. The show was designed to encourage debate. Opponents on the issue sat across from one another with the host in the middle. Before long charges and countercharges were flying.

Details of the incident concerning little Pete were aired with neither side giving ground. But as the end of the program neared, the foster mother supporting the agency—a woman who had cared for about fifty foster children over the years—was asked how she had become involved with such a large number of kids.

"Oh, we care for them a while, and then we send them on to some other nice home," she replied.

None of the participants on the air picked up on her remark—and it was, no doubt, an innocent comment spoken by a sincere, loving woman. But the implication of her statement enraged me. I yelled back at the TV set, "That's the problem, you idiots! How can any kid feel loved and secure when he's bounced from home to home?"

I was still fuming after the show ended. I introduced myself to the lady from the agency. I was blunt.

"You don't know me. My name is Glenn Hester. I'm a former foster child from your agency. I'm one of the survivors of your concentration camp, Pinewood Farms. I can't believe this garbage is still goin' on. Do you know how close foster kids come to bein' murdered, their pride and hope executed?"

The woman was startled, not sure how to respond to me. I calmed down, and we talked for a few minutes and finally agreed to meet some other time for more discussion of foster care.

After this experience with the Donnellys, I began to study the foster care system in New York and across the country. In a way foster care did not concern me anymore; I had escaped to adulthood. I had my own life to live. I had my job, and I wanted to spend time with Carla, strengthening our own home. But I could not forget the innocent face of little Pete, his curly black hair ringing those soft, dark eyes.

My research continued. I visited local government offices, checked out resources at the library, and followed the media for any news on foster care. It wasn't long before I concluded that foster care was a national disgrace. The problem for the most part was not with foster parents, but with the private agencies that are given control of the children by the courts. In fact without the loving dedication of thousands of foster parents, who are usually underpaid and receive few thanks from anyone for what they do, it seemed to me foster care in America would better be called "foster war." What better word than *war* is there for a system that devastates many helpless children?

I learned that children often are shuffled away from natural parents into foster care too soon, shifted from foster home to foster home too frequently, and stay in uneasy limbo in foster care too long.

A typical scenario for a foster child is the following: For one of many reasons the family court becomes aware that a particular child is being neglected or abused by his natural parent or parents. The court decides it would be best for the child to be removed from the home and placed with foster parents in a typical two-parent family home, in a group home, or in an institution. Some agency must administer this procedure, often a private organization that recruits and trains foster parents and locates parents for adoptable kids. In return the agency receives a government subsidy for each child.

All of this sounds harmless and compassionate, and some agencies do a thoroughly professional job, rendering a great service to children. Frequently, though, these private agencies develop an entrenched bureaucracy, a body of employees relying on maintaining a certain number of children on government subsidy to continue the "business."

Nationwide, the average annual government payment

per child to agencies is $7,000. This is the *average*. For kids with handicaps or special problems, the payment may reach $25,000 or higher. If an agency places a child for adoption, the government pays the agency a one-time fee, possibly as high as $3,000, usually much less. It's easy to see why for "mysterious reasons" most child care agencies have a very poor record in placing kids for adoption.

For example, in New York City, seventy-eight percent of the children in foster care who are cleared for adoption are still waiting to be placed. An agency's profit-loss picture is much rosier if a large number of foster kids are maintained.

Of course, there are expenses in keeping kids. Some of the government subsidy must be paid to foster parents. But these payments are normally low, and national studies have shown that fifty percent of the tax money supplied for each child goes for salaries of social workers and maintenance of organizations.

The cost of foster care is enormous. It is estimated that federal and state governments spend as high as 1.5 billion dollars a year on the estimated 500,000 foster kids in the United States. In New York City alone, over 300 million tax dollars are spent on 24,000 foster children each year.

The more I learned, the more I pestered public officials with letters and phone calls. And I sought every opportunity to speak my mind through the media.

Months passed and during a business slump in late 1978, National Car Rental laid me off. Jobs were scarce, so I decided it would be wise to gain even more technical skills. I applied for another education loan and enrolled in a welding course so I could be a good, all-purpose repairman. Carla wasn't too excited about more months of squeezing our budget, but she agreed my education would be a good investment in our future.

One evening in March, 1979, Carla and I drove to Newark Airport to pick up our pastor, who was returning from a trip. Carla was glad to get me away from the apartment for a few hours. Of late I had been preparing to testify before a state hearing on foster care and was unbearably preoccupied. The plane was not on time, so we sat down at the gate waiting area, catching up on small talk. I was glad, too, to have my mind diverted; but as a familiar-looking man walked by, my attention was wrenched back to foster care in a disturbingly personal way.

The man passed by, oblivious to us, but my heart began to pound and my fists clenched. I had told Carla many times that when I was younger—long before I became a Christian—there was one man on earth I had sworn to kill. Many, many years had gone by since I first made that vow, and in the meantime I had never seen him. But there he was, walking slowly away down a long hall at Newark Airport.

"Carla! It's Williams from Pinewood," I gasped. At first I couldn't move. My longed-for moment of revenge had come, but I no longer lived for revenge. I wasn't sure what to do.

I chased after him. As she watched me go, Carla began to worry. She knew how much I had hated Williams and his school. As I ran I considered my options. My blood was running hot, and I wanted to knock him out cold. I noticed, though, that the airport terminal was well patrolled by policemen.

"Mr. Williams, Mr. Williams, hey, is that you?" I called. He stopped, turning as I reached him. "Do you remember me, Mr. Williams? From Pinewood Farms? I'm Glenn Hester. I was one of your boys there." I stopped speaking, breathless.

He looked at me, puzzled, the faintest glimmer of fear in his eyes. I could tell he didn't know who I was. His sober, undramatic reaction to me snuffed the flames of my anger. I gazed at the man, knowing immediately I wasn't the same Glenn Hester who had yearned for his blood. Williams still represented, more than any other person, the brutality of my childhood. But I didn't hate him anymore. I saw him for what he was, an aging man, his eyes dull, his face gray and sad, his flesh drooping on his frame.

We visited awkwardly for a moment. It was obvious

neither of us was overly nostalgic about Pinewood Farms. He said that he had left the place years ago. We parted. He walked on to his plane. I walked back to Carla, my legs wobbly from emotion.

Back at our apartment, when I thought some more about my chance meeting with Williams, I began to cry. I was relieved and happy, aware again of how much the love of Christ had changed me. I knew for certain I truly was a new person and no longer a prisoner of my old hatreds.

April, 1979, came. The flowers bloomed, the grass greened—but I scarcely noticed. My appearance as a former foster child at the state commission hearing was approaching, and I had to prepare my testimony.

I did some more research, learning that in the United States, while an estimated 1.5 billion government dollars are spent each year on foster care, only 56 million dollars are expended to prevent family breakup—often the first event for kids destined for foster homes. Then, after entering foster care, the children are supervised by social workers who often are young, inexperienced, underpaid, and overworked. I found that although the recommended number of children per social worker is twenty to thirty, the actual nationwide average is seventy to ninety.

This overburdening of personnel helped clarify for me why the cases of many kids never receive any kind of systematic review. Some authorities believe that because of understaffing, as many as one third of all kids in foster care are, in effect, lost and forgotten. No one has time to keep track of them.

The day of the hearing arrived; I groomed myself carefully and put on my suit. I caught the subway to Manhattan and found the hearing room in city hall. I was early, so I took a seat near the back and listened to several speakers. Those testifying and commenting—the social workers, representatives of care agencies, psychiatrists, foster parents—all spoke sincerely and impressively; facts and figures filled the room. But it seemed to me they were dancing around the issues, afraid to point a finger of blame. No one wanted to say that a large number of private foster care agencies were using innocent kids as products in a booming, profit-making business financed by taxpayers. This irritated me, and when my turn came to testify, I attacked.

I read from a statement I had prepared, beginning by briefly telling my story. When I told of being bumped from foster homes to orphanages to institutions—in the process being severely abused—a few eyes lifted in the hearing room. I told how my moving from place to place had destroyed my trust to the point that at age nine a psychiatrist had diagnosed me as a child who neither loved nor trusted anyone. I told of my mental disorders and my experiences as an institutionalized mental patient.

"I feel I was suffering from mental illness caused by my ill-fated experiences as a foster child," I charged.

I wrapped up my history, revealing how my life had been changed after I was born again through belief in Jesus Christ.

Then I asked some pointed questions: "How is it that a professional agency, such as the one holding me in care, could allow such a chain of events to happen to me as well as to others?

"Why has no real investigation ever been made or criminal charges of child neglect or abuse brought against individuals in this agency?

"When it was obvious that my mother didn't want the responsibility of caring for me, why wasn't I placed for adoption?

"I could have had parents to love me and the security of a home of my own. . . ."

My allotted time for testimony expired. I answered a few questions and left. I was happy to have spoken out but relieved it was over.

Several months later in the fall, another newspaper article jarred me almost as much as the one on Pete had many months before. On October 8, I read that the chairman of the New York City Council, Carol Bellamy, had told the press that eighteen of New York City's children in foster care had already died that year, five of them as a result of maltreatment. This was just in New York City. I wondered how many others across America had died or were still suffering?

I thought about Pete again, wondering how he was doing. Would he survive? And if he did, would his future include a mental institution or a prison cell?

I decided I had to do more. Somehow I had to convince people that there are thousands of foster kids in this country who need help and love. I had to spread the message that this decrepit, ineffective, rotten foster care system is destroying the lives of kids, and somebody needs to stop it.

I prayed. An idea came. I decided to tell my story in a book. You've just read it. Those kids are waiting, waiting for you and me to do something.